Fly
Into the
Wind

ALSO BY LT COLONEL DAN ROONEY

A Patriot's Calling: My Life as an F-16 Fighter Pilot

Fly Into the Wind

How to Harness Faith and Fearlessness on Your Ascent to Greatness

Lt Colonel Dan "Noonan" Rooney

HARPER LARGE PRINT

An Imprint of HarperCollinsPublishers

HarperCollins books may be purchased for educational, business, or sales promotional use. For information, please e-mail the Special Markets Department at SPsales@harpercollins.com.

FIRST HARPER LARGE PRINT EDITION

ISBN: 978-0-06-297898-1

Library of Congress Cataloging-in-Publication Data is available upon request.

20 21 22 23 24 LSC 10 9 8 7 6 5 4 3 2 1

To my girls: Jacqy, Victoria, Tatum, Mia, Reese, and Devyn. Thank you for your unwavering support.

Contents

Foreword

I will never forget the day I flew with Lieutenant Colonel Dan "Noonan" Rooney, although I have every excuse, as I had been knocked unconscious that very morning. I was riding my bike uphill and out of the saddle (and, ironically, "into the damn wind"), when two idiots came hurtling downhill around a corner and plowed head on into me. I don't know how long I was unconscious, but when I came out of the ether, my very first thought was "Noonan must not know of this." You see, not everyone gets to fly in the back seat of an F-16 Viper, and I knew if he or the flight surgeon ever got wind of what was definitely a concussion (or the fact that for several hours I didn't know whether I was blown up or stuffed) my chance would be gone.

It was the 2007 PGA Championship at Southern Hills in Tulsa, and I was there working the event for CBS. Growing up in Northern Ireland, surrounded by soldiers, I had an affinity for the military, and ever since 9/11, something had ached inside of me. I had lived in America since 1993, had fallen in love with the place, and I couldn't bear the thought of terrorism reaching the shores of yet another place I thought of as home. When Dan described his vision for Folds of Honor and asked if I would help in promoting the launch of the foundation, I jumped at the chance, to say the least. Our troops had our backs downrange, and this was a chance to do something for their families if they didn't make it home.

It was well over 100 degrees Fahrenheit that afternoon, and after three hours of ingress and egress education (none of which got past the concussion), I put on my harness, which connects me to the ejection seat, and tightened the straps. *How the hell is he walking upright?* I thought, as I walked like a crippled lobster behind Dan, across the sweltering apron, toward that beautiful machine. He turned around, giggling, and said, "You don't tighten up until you get in the seat, you moron." *Right, I knew that.* "You know all that ingress and egress stuff you just sat through?" he said.

"Uh-huh." I nodded.

"Forget it, just don't touch anything yellow."

As it turned out, the ejection handle under my seat was yellow. Enough said. I loosened my straps and did my best Tom Cruise swagger to the bottom of the ladder, climbed up, and shoehorned myself into the back seat. Not a lot of room.

At the time, my daily driver was a Porsche 911 Turbo, so I didn't think I'd be freaked out by the airplane's acceleration down the runway. Math was never my strong suit, so I don't know how many times a 911 Turbo goes into 29,000 pounds of thrust. Suffice to say that we hadn't gone a nine iron's length down the runway before I wanted my mommy. Everyone had told me that I should eat a banana before I did this, as bananas taste the same coming up as they do going down, but I dislike being told what to do, so I'd had a big sweaty cheeseburger and a chocolate malt for lunch. That was beginning to feel like a bad decision.

I have no idea what speed we were doing when Dan pointed that damn thing vertical, but I felt the change of direction in my dental work, and that was just the beginning. Once we were at 20,000 feet, Dan pulled the F-16 on its back and rolled over. I felt like some idiot had touched something yellow, and I was being catapulted out of the canopy. Nothing, and I mean *nothing*, can prepare a layperson for the violence of such an experience, and it was right then that I started to wonder if the crazy idiot in front of me was a human being. *No normal person could do this for a living,* I thought, as my testicles snapped back into place. If I'd known that *that* was going to happen, I would have bought them a little G-suit of their own.

What an hour of my life that was. We pulled nine Gs twice, I didn't pass out, and the cheeseburger didn't come out of either end of me! We rocketed over the clubhouse at Southern Hills at what seemed like about 13 feet high, and when Dan said it was time to land, I squealed like a little boy, "Noooooooooo!" It was too much fun! But CBS had documented the whole thing, and Folds of Honor was up and running. I was right about one thing: Lt Colonel Dan Rooney is no ordinary person.

A few weeks later, I called Dan and asked how I could get my then-Irish ass to Iraq. He pulled a few levers (none of them yellow), and the following year, I was there with the USO, a trip that changed my life forever. I came back wanting—no, *needing*—to be an American. And I did: I became a U.S. citizen and even started my own foundation, Troops First.

It takes a special person to give an alcoholic drug addict in the throes of mental illness the opportunity to have such an experience, but if you read this book you'll get it, just like I did, and you will find yourself equipped with the tools to make your life and the lives of those around you better. Dan Rooney is a special friend to me and was an inspiration at a time in my life when I thought I had no purpose.

Noonan's fighter-pilot mind can process information at extraordinary speeds. This gives him the unique ability to see details and dimensions that most people never notice. *Fly Into the Wind* is the awesome culmination of Lt Colonel Dan's study of life. His single-seat-fighter-pilot mentality drives his ethos that one person can trigger enormous change and impact. His personal struggles taught him that in order to ascend, we need to feel pressure on the underside of our wings, and to have the strength to hold those wings steady in the storm. Dan has found that strength in his faith, and in common sense too. Every player on the PGA Tour knows that it's easier to find that difficult flag, the one just over the bunker, if you have the wind in your face. Downwind gets you nowhere near, and nothing in life is valuable without the challenge that comes before it.

—David Feherty

Author's Note

Four hundred and eighty knots appeared on my head-up display as the mountains rising from the Arizona desert flew past my canopy. When we fly 500 feet AGL (above ground level) the time to die (hit the ground) is less than two seconds in the F-16. Pilots break down the dynamic arena of low-level flying into three distinct parts to help us prioritize—*near rocks, far rocks . . . check six.* As I cruised along the terra firma, this hallowed advice recirculated in my mind. *Near rocks* represent danger close, such as towers or surface-to-air missiles. *Far rocks* expand the mental telescope to the threats farther down the low-level route. *Check six* refers to unexpected bogeys (enemy aircraft) that may sneak up behind you. Sudden change is a constant in the fast jet business, but it teaches us to control our emotions, evaluate the situation, and take appropriate action.

Sudden change hit our world in 2020. Given the events of COVID-19, I would be remiss not to share a little perspective. First, I offer my prayers for those who have died. Beyond the incalculable loss of life, most of us left behind have faced very real financial and emotional struggles. These effects are hard to comprehend when you think that no one currently living has a reference point for a situation this catastrophic. Despite these challenges, I believe there has been a true blessing bestowed on the world. God continues to reaffirm that HE is the pilot in command. Overnight, most of the important stuff that filled our daily lives stopped. The human race actually slowed down. Some of us were given the rare gift of time to reflect on our ordinarily busy lives, but all of us were thrust into an unfamiliar world in which is hidden an opportunity to reimagine our lives and our new normal.

Fly Into the Wind was scheduled for publication in April but was delayed by the unexpected disruption of coronavirus. *Check six!* However, as you will discover in these pages, I firmly believe that God puts challenges in our path to help us evolve. I embrace challenges as a sort of life vector, and use them to alter my course.

When fighter pilots fly at low level, we intentionally plot the route with a few "get-well points," large landmarks such as a lake or highway we affectionately refer to as "dog-balls" because you can't miss them. If your ground track or timing is off, you can use these points as a course correction. COVID-19 was a get-well point for much of humanity, allowing us to realign and reprioritize. Offering you a code of living to help you find your new normal and a better way of life, *Fly Into the Wind* is the perfect book for this season of humanity. My prayer for all of us is that we don't forget the lessons learned and the get-well opportunity that COVID-19 has given us.

Fly
Into the
Wind

1
Broken Wings

The sky was the color of perfection that morning, steel blue that stretched out for miles over the vast beige and burnt green pastures of Oklahoma. Pilots refer to a sky as majestic as this one as CAVU, or "ceiling and visibility unrestricted"—the ideal conditions for flying. Rare to achieve but impossible not to appreciate. When I walked over to the F-16, climbed up the ladder, and strapped myself in that day, I had never felt better. I had just returned safely from my third tour of duty in Iraq and looked forward to a routine sortie, a basic training flight, free from the dangers of the war zone.

Brave 1, cleared onto hold 18 left.

I gently pushed the throttle forward with my left hand and taxied the F-16, or "Viper," as those who fly call it, onto the runway. I aligned my jet in a side-by-side formation with my flight lead, and we waited for takeoff clearance. Once airborne, I would rejoin into a fingertip formation, a mere three feet separating our wingtips. Flying so closely would be incredibly dangerous in the world of traditional aviation, but the fighter-pilot nation is anything but traditional. There's an unparalleled level of precision and trust that permeates our world.

As I waited for takeoff clearance, my eyes systematically scanned the LED screens and vast number of dials, ensuring all systems were in the green. The Pratt & Whitney 229 engine growled below me. *Brave 1, wind 190 at 13, cleared for takeoff 18 left,* came over the radio. My flight lead gave me a quick salute, and I watched the rapid line of sight of his F-16 taking off into the wind. I followed exactly ten seconds later, moving the throttle to afterburner. The snarling beast came to life with a chest-pounding 29,000 pounds of thrust, more horsepower than the entire starting grid at the Daytona 500. Within seconds, I was yet again living my boyhood dream and slipping the surly bonds of earth in my single-seat fighter jet. CAVU, and the feeling of transcendence that accompanies it, was mine.

An hour later, we returned from the bombing range in southern Oklahoma to our base in Tulsa. It was an uneventful sortie, but I was happy to win a few bucks in the bet I had made with my flight lead. I had dropped my practice bombs—"sport bombing," as we affectionately call it—and shot the M61 cannon★ more accurately than he had.

After the morning go, the crew chiefs and support team refueled the jets, loaded up ordnance,† and performed other required maintenance to ensure that the jets were code one for the afternoon missions. As they were doing so, a command came over the intercom: "Noonan, please report to ops desk." Noonan is the call sign that was given to me by my fellow pilots. It was inspired by the fact that I am the only person in the world to be both a PGA Professional and an Air Force fighter pilot, and, yes, it comes from the character in the classic comedy *Caddyshack*. It was my crew chief on the phone, who asked that I come look at the jet I had flown that morning. This wasn't a typical request. My pulse raced as I walked to the flight line.

★ The M61 20mm Vulcan is an externally powered six-barrel rotary-fire gun with a rate of fire of up to 100 rounds per second.
† That's how we refer to the bombs on board our jets.

What does he want to show me? Is something wrong?
Or scarier yet: *Did I do something wrong?*

"Noonan, did you see this?" my crew chief asked.
He pointed to the centerline external fuel tank, where a
slow drip of jet fuel was leaking from the bottom of my
jet, right below the 370-gallon tank. My heart dropped.
I knew instantly what had happened.

Let me first say this: The F-16 is no ordinary plane.
As opposed to other jets, it goes airborne within seconds. Capable of reaching a top speed of 1,400 miles
per hour (Mach 2.4)—that's going from Los An-
geles to San Diego or Dallas to Austin in about four
minutes—the F-16 can climb straight up to 50,000 feet
in less than one minute. Because of this extraordinary
power, the flaps on the F-16 are computerized as part
of a complex fly-by-wire system. On a commercial jet,
the pilot will move the flap actuator by hand once the
plane has enough lift and is far enough away from the
ground. The Viper has so much thrust that the flight
control computer automatically retracts the flaps when
the gear handle is raised to prevent them from being
oversped, or damaged from exceeding maximum
speed. When the flaps go up, lift is reduced and the jet
sinks just slightly.

The tapes, once pulled, confirmed what I had expected. It was 100 percent pilot error—*my error.* I had

prematurely retracted the landing gear, which caused the jet to settle back down on the external gas tank and scrape against the runway. Had the tank dragged even a fraction of a second longer, there's a good chance those 370 gallons of jet fuel would have exploded underneath me. You don't need to be an engineer to realize that mistake could've been the end of the jet, and quite possibly the end of me. I had survived in the most dangerous, war-torn places on earth, having performed my duties at the highest level in Iraq, only to narrowly escape a disaster due to my own negligence.

This mistake was a serious chink in my armor. Upon returning home as a two-time Top Gun award recipient, I was being groomed to attend Fighter Weapons School at Nellis Air Force Base in Las Vegas. I was positioned, destined even, for a very promising military career. As I drove home that evening, I reflected on how the years of hard work I had put into becoming a pilot were nearly extinguished in seconds.

Until that day, my life had been like a series of puzzle pieces that, for the most part, had happily clicked into place. As a kid growing up in Oklahoma, my ambitions knew no bounds. As a little guy, I was always drawn to machines—from my mother's Kirby vacuum that I pushed around as soon as I could walk, to our faded green John Deere 110 tractor that I got cleared solo on at the age of eight to cut the lawn. I strived for perfection even then, wanting the Bermudagrass at our house on 2624 Black Oak Drive to look like Augusta National. My older sisters, Beth and Kate, were great company, but as the only boy I had to find my own fun. My energy levels put me in perpetual motion, and the only thing that made me stop was hearing the whine of a jet engine flying over me at 31,000 feet. I'd squint up from underneath the brim of my sweat-stained baseball cap, mesmerized by the white contrails that crisscrossed in the boundless sky.

I was hardwired for it. My Grandpa Rooney was deployed after the attack on Pearl Harbor and was stationed at Bury St. Edmunds north of London from 1942 to 1945, then became director of the Illinois Air National Guard until his retirement after thirty years of service. I admired the faded black-and-white photograph of "Grampie" in full military dress, the silver eagle on his uniform denoting his rank of colonel. His storied military career fascinated me, and I let my imagination run wild with images of war heroes fighting against the axis of evil. Though I was a few decades removed from the Nazis, I wanted nothing more than to be part of the brave and chivalrous fraternity that was charged with defending our great nation. But since I was obviously too young to join the Air Force, I dedicated myself to my first dream of playing golf at its highest level.

I was five when my dad started letting me tag along with his regular golf game, and it was he who cut down a five-wood, five-iron, wedge, and putter to my size and gave me a few Titleist balls to try my skills on. By the time I was ten, my parents dropped me at the course in the morning, my clubs and a swimsuit being all I needed to occupy me for the full day. At twelve, I got my first job working as a "range rat" for my local PGA Pro at Stillwater Country Club. Collecting range balls in the heat and dust taught me much about the power of hard work and perseverance, but there was an encounter that summer that would have a monumental impact on my life. That was the fateful summer I met Steve "Reno" Cortright, a fighter pilot in the Oklahoma Air National Guard, while he was playing in the Sigma Chi golf tournament. Steve was the prototypical fighter pilot—good-looking, with a jock swagger and confidence that bordered on arrogance. The original *Top Gun* movie had just come out, and several viewings combined with my meeting Reno convinced me there was no greater career path than becoming a fighter pilot. But that dream would have to wait a little longer.

As a teenager, I grew much more serious about my golf game, practicing in the 100-plus-degree heat of an Oklahoma summer. I routinely hit golf balls until my hands bled, but it paid off: I became a top player at the University of Kansas, where I received a golf scholarship. After graduation, I moved to Florida and hit the mini-tour circuits playing professional golf. I'd soon learn that while grit and tenacity were essential to reaching my dream, so was money. In order to get into Air Force flight school, I'd have to meet the prerequisite of getting a pilot's license, which meant paying for flying lessons. Each tournament check got me a little bit closer to being able to rent a plane for lessons.

When I finally had enough saved up, I was able to rent a Cessna 152, which resembled a tin can with a propeller and wings. If I was flying into a south wind, the traffic on the highway below me would be traveling faster. I loved flying the Cessna at 95 miles per hour, but I couldn't stop thinking about what it would be like to fly the Viper. I couldn't wait to have the chance to beat gravity into submission.

Soon after getting my pilot's license, I signed my marriage license with my soul mate, Jacqy. We met our freshman year at the University of Kansas when she showed up for a date with my roommate at the Sigma Chi house. Luckily for me, things didn't work out with her and my roommate, and we started dating a few months later. I'm proud to say that we've now been together for twenty-seven years.

We had been married for six months when we got a lottery ticket that would change our lives forever. It wasn't good for money, but it was good for one boyhood dream: One of the greatest days of my life was when I was accepted into the Undergraduate Pilot Training (UPT) program, where I'd be faced with some of the military's most grueling training. Truth be told, my chances of making it through were slim. A mere 4.8 percent of pilots in the U.S. Air Force will complete the fighter jet training program, meaning the remaining 95 percent will default on their dreams. Perhaps even more staggering is the fact that over a ten-year period, more people will play in the National Football League than will fly a fighter jet. If playing for the NFL sounds like a laughable dream, it turns out that becoming a fighter pilot is even more ridiculous.

The Air Force spends approximately $6 million to mint one fighter pilot in a two-and-a-half-year-long training program. On our first day of training, the colonel informed us that while we "had the opportunity of a lifetime," we should prepare for "the best and worst days of our lives." He wasn't kidding. The experience was demanding, exhausting, and often utterly frustrating. But it was also exhilarating. I entered flight school with a mere sixty hours of flying time in a little Cessna, and just eight months later I was flying supersonic in a T-38. After thirteen months of training, I left Wichita Falls, Texas, with wings confidently displayed on my chest.

The setting sun burned my eyes as Jacqy, our two dogs, and I headed to Luke Air Force Base in Glendale, Arizona, for nine months in the Formal Training Unit (FTU), where I would, *finally*, learn to fly the F-16! All these years later, I still have trouble putting that experience into words. I can still envision myself as a little boy standing on my parents' land, marveling at the white contrails, thinking how high they were and how fast they moved.

Life moves at an incredibly fast pace too. While stationed at Luke AFB, Jacqy and I welcomed our first daughter, Victoria, into our world. I finished my F-16 training and immediately deployed on the first of what would be three tours of duty to Iraq. Leaving my young family was always the hardest part of combat. It's like momentarily stepping outside your life and not being able to do anything about the consequences. Thankfully, I made it home safely from my first deployment.

In 2007, after my second tour of Iraq, I would be called on another mission, this time to launch the Folds of Honor Foundation in the humble space above my garage. My dream for Folds was to provide scholarships to the dependents of our military who had lost their lives or had been gravely injured in service to our country. Thanks to the support of PGA of America and golfers across the country, Folds was soon going vertical, raising a million dollars in its first year of operation alone. Not only was I giving back to the armed forces, which had given me my boyhood dream, but I was working alongside my dad to build a golf club in Tulsa, Oklahoma, called The Patriot. The Patriot was going to be a world-class golf course, as well as the future Folds of Honor headquarters, designed by the famous Robert Trent Jones Jr. My life had manifested in beautiful ways I could never have imagined, but that was all about to change.

The simple act of raising the gear handle a second early was a near-fatal mistake, and in a strange twist of fate would trigger something much more ominous. I started to walk down a very dark path. I couldn't stop thinking about how I had survived war, only to make such a complacent mistake. I doubted myself and my own worth, and as these thoughts ran through my mind in a vicious circle, pulling me into a deeper void, I developed anxiety and depression. I was haunted by a constant state of fight or flight, consumed by a feeling of panic that wouldn't go away. At night I'd wake up in pouring sweat from a recurring nightmare—flying my F-16 down on the deck over the ocean and crashing without pulling the ejection handle. Mornings were equally scary, filled with a burning dread of having to get up and face the day. My positivity, energy, and mental health were in an emergency descent.

As my anxiety and depression persisted, everything else systematically began to come apart. Folds of Honor went from flourishing to teetering on the brink, and The Patriot was virtually destroyed by a hundred-year flood and the Great Recession. As a result, my finances were a disaster and bankruptcy hovered like a low-scud layer over my life. My marriage and family struggled because of all the external pressures. People whom I believed I could count on walked away. And for the first time in my life, I felt alone and hopeless.

If I thought the incident with my gear would be the worst day of my career, I was wrong. Three years later, on what would go down as one of the worst days of my life, I slowly tightened the laces of my flight boots, knowing it would be the last time I did so. Based on the perilous trajectory of Folds of Honor and The Patriot, I had no choice. I somberly walked into my squadron commander's office and quit being a fighter pilot. As I left the office, I realized that it had taken ten years to hone my skills as an F-16 pilot, but only a couple of minutes to turn my back on flying Vipers and a promising military career. I had put everything I had into recognizing this boyhood dream of flying F-16s—flying had become my touchstone, something I could always count on—and now it was gone.

I continued to struggle over the next few years. Despite my best efforts, Folds and The Patriot were still in jeopardy. With nothing left to give, I hit rock bottom. I prayed for intervention. The easy out was to leave Folds of Honor and settle into a more conventional life as an airline pilot. And I had one boot out the door, ready to do so, when a small ray of light pierced my darkness.

I was playing golf in Grand Haven, Michigan, on Patriot Golf Day—Folds of Honor's national fundraiser—when I met Carlos Seise, an avid golfer and world-class opera singer who was there to compete as well as regale the crowd with "God Bless America." There is something powerful about playing a round of golf with another person, be it a stranger or someone you've known for years; golf creates a fellowship unique among sports. On that day, I got to know Carlos and opened up to him about the difficult crossroads I was facing. We were standing on the green of the thirteenth hole and I was explaining my situation when Carlos said, "I believe you have been chosen by

God for this work, and you must stay the course." I wasn't convinced, but then Carlos said, "We're on the thirteenth hole. Do you know the real meaning of the number 13?"

"Yes . . . it ties back to the thirteen folds that make the American flag triangle shape."

"That may be true, but the real meaning ties to the Bible," he said. "There are twelve apostles, plus Jesus. Thirteen is the number of new beginnings."

I let what he had just told me sink in and felt the Holy Spirit wash over me. *New beginnings.* Then I asked myself: *Do I have the power to create a new chapter in my life?* That day with Carlos was a gift from God, and thereafter four things soon became clear:

1. There was no quick fix to my situation.

2. Life is about much more than being happy.

3. If I live the life that God calls me to, I will find fulfillment.

4. I was being prepared for something bigger on the other side of my storm.

Being exposed to that ray of hope on the thirteenth hole that day helped me accept that my current circumstances were beyond my control, but that I also had a choice. I could fight each wave that hit me until I was exhausted and empty, or I could pray, practice patience, and look for a vector out of the storm. I could start seeking fulfillment rather than trying to fix the brokenness in my life.

Over the course of a decade-long period of struggle and introspection and subsequent resolution, I developed a personal code of living that I call CAVU. It is made up of ten unique and powerful lines of effort (LOEs).* This code of living has changed the aperture of my life, widening my focus to reveal a portal that opens to a much bigger world. CAVU is about operating from a place of purpose—it's about moving through life as an open vessel and being receptive to its various effects, be they good or bad.

No storm lasts forever. Eventually the downpour becomes a light mist, and dark skies crack open to reveal the smallest hint of light. CAVU emerges, a sky sparkling in a brilliant shade of the sharpest blue. I stand stronger after facing my personal challenges head on and now understand that I have been blessed

---

* In a military campaign, LOEs represent a coalition of forces, personnel, and weapon systems that are strategically used to create the greatest impact

with a true gift. I have the ultimate flying conditions *for life.*

It took four years before I got a second chance on a once-in-a-lifetime dream. I was in Arlington, Virginia, when I met General Mark A. Welsh III, the chief of staff of the U.S. Air Force. His job was to organize, train, and equip 660,000 airmen, but he cared enough about me to ask why I had left the Air Force. I shared my story and the fact that my life was now headed in a positive direction. When General Welsh encouraged me to come back, all of my hesitations fell away. I knew I was ready to fly again.

I have been back flying fighters for almost six years. Meanwhile, Folds of Honor has awarded more than twenty-five thousand scholarships to military dependents and The Patriot is thriving. Most importantly, on the back side of the storm I emerged as a much better person, dedicated to life based upon a daily code of living. There's a new mission I've been tasked with, and that's sharing CAVU with you.

YOUR PATH FORWARD

Wherever you are right now is exactly where you're supposed to be. If you are already thriving, CAVU can help you continue your ascent. Or if you're like I was—

surrounded by darkness and despair, hopelessness and adversity—CAVU can help you break through to the other side and achieve a life you've never imagined. I am aware that there are many degrees of struggle (many of them worse than mine), but in a world that often seems divided, struggle is our common denominator.

You've undoubtedly heard stories about big failures preceding epic successes. Teddy Roosevelt overcame debilitating childhood illnesses to live a life of valor and courage, and he remains the youngest person to become president of the United States. Francis "Gabby" Gabreski was told by his military instructor that he "did not have the touch to be a pilot," but went on to become the only ace in both World War II and the Korean War. And then there's John McCain, who was a POW for over six years in Vietnam and was subjected to brutal torture. Rather than letting himself be crushed by the horrors of war, McCain returned home and became a congressman and a long-term senator, ran for president, and died in 2018 an American hero.

These are extreme examples, of course, but we can all point to people around us—our family members, our friends, our neighbors, our bosses—who make success look easy. This is especially true in a society dominated by social media, where it's easy to think life is a never-ending series of high-five moments and personal achievements. We hear about the victories, not the struggles. But similar to how a fighter jet takes off into the wind because the resistance is essential for liftoff, our lives should be no different. The challenges in our lives are not there to keep us down, but rather to help us ascend.

This book will prepare you to live a better life, but to be clear, this isn't a book about being happy. A quick internet search will show you countless options for books on happiness, but happiness is fleeting, and emotions rarely fall within the domain of our control. This book is about being *Full-Filled*. Being fulfilled provides the ultimate foundation from which to thrive, grow, enjoy, and appreciate everything life has to offer. I hope that by implementing what I learned during my storm, you will be renewed with the energy to move forward and face life's challenges with integrity and strength.

Understand that if you want to chase the big dreams in your heart, you will likely be crushed at some point during the journey. That's okay. There are evil spirits that prowl about the world and thrive on keeping you down, but make no mistake: What you do when things don't go your way defines who you really are. Right now, are you ultimately the person you want to be? Do you want to be more fulfilled, more passionate, have more energy to be more impactful? Are you alive, or *are you just living*?

It is my honor and privilege to share the steps I've taken to become a more faithful servant of God, engaged and fulfilled husband, father, son, brother, philanthropist, leader, fighter pilot, PGA Pro, and friend. My promise to you is that I will remain open and honest as your humble servant. I will be your advocate as you explore CAVU and learn to apply ten lines of effort so you can conquer your divine mission in life, whatever that may be. You were made for it!

RULES OF ENGAGEMENT (ROE)

Let's cover the ROE before we start.

As fighter pilots, we learn in a very process-driven environment, one that has been honed and refined over generations. While this isn't going to teach you how to fly a fighter jet, the instructional progression in this book is inspired by one of the most efficient teaching processes the world has ever known. A critical piece of our learning process involves the "three Cs": clear, concise, correct comm (communication). We take great pride in efficient communication in the fighter-pilot community. My goal with each evolution (chapter) is to clearly define an LOE in a *high-speed, low-drag* learning environment.

Each chapter will introduce you to some of my heroes, some of whom I have been blessed to call friends, and some of whom I have never met. Nevertheless, each has contributed to my code of living. Their heroic stories add depth and color to each LOE.

In the Air Force, we systematically debrief after every flight. In this tradition, I will chalk up the objectives and highlight lessons learned throughout the book. As your instructor (IP) it is my singular goal to help you achieve CAVU. In the words of Proverbs 27:17, *As iron sharpens iron, so one person sharpens another.*

Now let's kick the tires and light the fire.

2

Quintessence

Sometimes, wonderful things are born from the darkest of places. Genesis tells of God creating heaven and earth from the depths of chaos (*The earth was without form and void, and darkness was upon the face of the deep*), a description that is apt for our lives as well. As I discovered during the war in Iraq, in which I encountered the most devastating scenes in my long flying career, the foundation of CAVU is the lesson that good can come from chaos. In many cases, it *must*.

Fear begins before the war. Saying goodbye to my family before deployment is one of the most difficult things I must do, and no matter how many times I've done it, the emotions never cease. Before departing, I would walk quietly into my daughters' bedrooms, place kisses on their beautiful foreheads, and pray it isn't the last time I tuck them in. My wife, Jacqy, never gets used to the vacancy that comes with being a military spouse. She would drive me to the base, and during the ride we'd sit in the car silently, neither of us wanting to say a thing for fear of the conversation growing too animated. Everything is said without us having to say a word. Our love and appreciation for each other is never more apparent than during those silent drives. As I'd step out of the Jeep, my stomach would sink when the reality of where I was headed hit me full force. I'm always confident I'll return safely, but I can never really know for sure.

All of us will leave this world someday, but deployment is like a sneak preview of that moment. What's humbling, to me at least, is knowing that life will continue without me while I'm in combat. Homework and laundry still need to get done. Holidays and birthday parties will be attended. Regular life, with all its small joys and complications, will persist whether or not I'm present for it. You never realize how wonderful normal is until you don't have it anymore.

My new normal started when I pushed up the throttle of the F-16, taking off at precisely 0200 while my family and friends slept under a warm blanket of freedom, the jet's afterburners streaking like comets across the Tulsa sky.

Destination: Iraq.

When I landed in Balad, the reality of war was made instantly clear. As we taxied off the runway, we were greeted by the warning claxon indicating incoming mortar fire. Mortars were lobbed into the base nearly every day and with such frequency that Balad is known as "Mortaritaville." Balad Air Base is located approximately forty miles northeast of Baghdad. It was originally called Al-Baqr Air Base, but the United States took it from the Iraqi air force in 2003 and poured billions into the infrastructure. Today, it's like a very crowded small city of 28,000 people, where ops are happening 24/7 at the highest tempo. Fighter jets light up the air, Navy SEALs and special ops burst through gates to fight the ground battle, and Army troops bustle with plans of base defense. Off the battlefield, the chow hall, gym, and latrine are always packed full with soldiers during their brief respites from combat ops. But even on base, the activity of war never ceases. Soldiers are accustomed to dropping flat to the ground the instant they hear the warning claxon. The danger of the war isn't just happening outside the wire; it's happening inside it too.

As a deployed member of the 332d Air Expedition-ary Wing, I was part of the mission in Iraq to provide support to our heroes fighting the battle on the ground. Close air support (CAS) was our primary tasking, and it generally consisted of airstrikes against hostile forces that were operating in close proximity to our troops on the ground. Before each sortie we'd execute a mission brief as each flight was evaluated against several clearly defined objectives. The first mission objective was al-ways written in all capital letters in a perfectly straight line on a bright, clean whiteboard. This important re-minder simply read:

KILL AND SURVIVE

Though my body eventually adjusted to battle rhythm—what I called the pace of deployment—I never got used to the actualities of war itself.

One might think that the sights of dead or injured bodies or the sounds of explosions and shouting are what I remember most. But I will never forget war's distinct smell. With afternoon temperatures in Iraq reaching 125 degrees Fahrenheit, the earth smelled like it was cooking. Acrid smoke from burn pits rolled over the base in black waves. For security reasons, we burned everything in open pits, a terrible-smelling mixture of fuel, plastics, uniforms, rubber, decaying flesh, and medical waste.

The only smell that comforted me came from my jet. Each time I approached the F-16, the familiar smell of JP-8 (the special kind of fuel military jets use) wrapped around me like a welcoming hug. I thought of it as the smell of speed.

On rare days when I wasn't flying a combat sortie or acting as supervisor of flying (SOF) at one of the busiest and most dynamic airfields in the world, I volunteered at the hospital. I'd go wherever I was needed, which could have meant one day I was moving supplies and meeting incoming transports, and another was visiting with soldiers in the recovery room. A ceaseless flow of coalition forces, enemy combatants, and civilians caught in the crossfire of war were brought in for treatment.

Balad Air Base features the most sophisticated trauma hospital in the world. The surgeons and their teams develop new procedures and groundbreaking techniques that increase their chances of saving lives, and emergency rooms all over America use the trauma techniques pioneered in Balad. But the smell there was poignant, a dramatic rendering of blood, burned flesh, gunpowder, and powerful disinfectant. The hospital's emergency room floors were often covered in pools of blood, a reminder that freedom is never free.

No matter how well my senses became attuned to war, there were times when I needed to find peace, however ephemeral. Shortly after I arrived for this tour of duty, I located a place where I could find respite from the chaos of war: the roof of the 332nd fighter squadron building. It was the only place I could be completely alone, a rare occurrence on base. I sat on an old metal folding chair and observed the dust particles in the air as they shimmered in shades of red, white, and green across the runway. I watched the afterburner of an F-16 that had taken off and noticed that the sun was starting to rise on the eastern horizon. But even the miracle of dawn couldn't bring light to the darkness of war.

Back home, my wife and daughters would be winding down for the night. They would be gathering at the table for dinner, saying grace, and sharing a meal while recounting details of their day. Meanwhile, I took a breath and offered up a prayer, asking for clarity as the sounds of battle ricocheted around me. As I prayed, I thought about the physical disparity between where I was and the warm family life I had left behind. I wondered if I had made the right choice, if this is what I wanted out of my time on earth.

After a long time sitting in quiet reflection, I felt a presence about me. It wasn't the oppressive hand of war, but rather a soft and calming sensation. For a moment, war did not exist and I breathed easier. Then, a word I had never heard before came into my head, settling there comfortably. Like a whisper, it echoed:

"Quintessence"

I don't know why that word came to me or why it instantly soothed me, but I do believe that God often puts things within us for a reason. I had faith that this word was significant and felt a compelling desire to explore its meaning.

My focus was brought back to the present by the sound of a helicopter rotating to land behind our squadron. I climbed down from the rooftop, thinking about the new word as I headed into the alert shack. Booting up my laptop, I brushed the residue of sand and dust off the keyboard and searched for the word on the internet.

I learned that the great ancient Greek philosopher Aristotle was the first person to ponder quintessence. Dubbing it "the fifth element," he imagined it was quintessence that breathed life into the elements: air, earth, fire, and water. Quintessence was believed to be an invisible force that existed throughout the world, unseen by the human eye. It represented perfection—the ultimate, purest form of something. Quintessence is so powerful that the Greeks believed our human senses did not have the capacity to comprehend it. It's not just ancient philosophers who studied it either. In modern physics there's a theory that most of the energy of the universe is made up of quintessence, that two-thirds of the universe consists of this energy that we cannot see or touch.

"Quintessence" was simply a word I had conjured during my brief respite on a rooftop, but it would soon become my lifelong friend.

LOE #1: QUINTESSENCE

*"For I know the plans I have for you," declares
the Lord, "plans to prosper you and not to harm
you, plans to give you hope and a future."*
(Jeremiah 29:11)

Like every training program of the military, the road to CAVU is front-loaded. In other words, you are going to face the most difficult and complex concept first: exploring and connecting to your quintessence. This isn't a cut-and-dry operation but a lifelong pursuit devoid of black-and-white answers. When I recall that moment when I was sitting on that rooftop, surrounded by the sounds, smells, and sights of war, this phantom energy makes sense. War exposes us to one of the worst sides of humanity, but quintessence suggests that there is much more going on beyond the broken parts of our world.

This first line of effort is directly connected to one of the most intense times in my life. I was mired in a war zone, which I would escape unscathed, only to be thrown into a decade-long storm marked by self-doubt and despair. I'm here to tell you that contemplating my quintessence was crucial to my coming out the other side. If you want to achieve a life that's richer and more fulfilling than anything you could ever have imagined, you must connect to the essence of who *you are*, that is, your quintessence. Connecting with your quintessence means:

- Going beyond what's typically expected of your vocation. It's about leaving your mark on the world, taking risks, performing good tasks, and inspiring others with your passion and dedication.

- Trusting your inner voice. That "spiritual voice" is not something to be dismissed.

- Not letting fear or ego stop you from following your desired path. Don't be afraid to dissect any feelings of discomfort in your heart.

- Remaining open to change and growth at all times.

- Honoring your passions and talents by exploring them, appreciating them, and sharing them with the world.

- Living a life that is meaningful to you. You can't connect with your quintessence if you're worried about pleasing other people. Only *you know* what your divine mission really entails.

Take a Personal Inventory

In this hyperconnected world, we are under constant assault from all directions. We are fed messages about everything from how we should live and what we should buy to what we should look like and what vocations are considered meaningful. That is why it's imperative to take a personal inventory and assess if you are headed down the path toward your divine mission. Without self-awareness and a practice of self-inventory, external forces can dominate and deter the direction of your pursuit. To be clear, this isn't as simple as "being the best you can be." Quintessence is elusive, and following your divine mission is a process that requires deep introspection and self-reflection. There are plenty of people who are "successful," but who have failed to align with God's intention for their lives. Making piles of money might be great—it is certainly one example of how our society measures success—but if it doesn't align with your core belief system, you're cheating yourself out of ultimate contentment. Success can also be far from "sublime" or "perfect" if it's mired in unethical practices, ego, and greed. As you begin the process of tending to and nurturing your quintessence, use the following questions to guide you through a personal inventory:

1. Deep in your gut, what do you feel you're intended to do? What are your deepest passions, desires, and talents?

2. What are your core beliefs? What qualities do you believe are crucial to being a faithful, productive servant of God? Are both your personal and business interactions aligned with your core beliefs? How can you better align them?

3. Are you being led by fear or ego? Are you making choices based on what society expects of you, or what you believe will lead to an easy win? Stop worrying about the what-ifs and tap into the creative portion of your brain. Like quintessence itself, your life is full of endless possibility.

Make a Plan and Hit Your Target

In its simplest form, one mission of the fighter pilot is to put bombs on time on target (BOTOT). Fighter pilots typically spend an entire day planning for a sortie that can last as long as ten hours (in combat) or as little as one to one and a half hours (in training). Regardless of whether we're in combat or flying a standard training sortie, our planning remains deliberate and exact. We target whatever our Combined Air Operations Center (CAOC) determines to be the priority, and the information we receive from them dictates our time on target (TOT). Everything is planned; the stakes are too high and too important for anything less than total preparation.

After every sortie, we debrief, which is an opportunity to grow and learn from any mistakes we might have made during our mission. We analyze whether we hit our targets. If we didn't, then why not? If we did, what went right? And what could be done better next time? The debriefing process is essential to the essence of my work as a fighter pilot. It's crucial to continually monitor my actions to stay safe, do a good job, be able to teach other pilots, and, if necessary, protect my country from harm.

Connecting with your own quintessence utilizes the same constant debriefing process. Continually monitor your life to see if you're orbiting around your core priorities. But most important, be honest with yourself. It's not unusual for our actions to be incongruent with what we believe or say is important in our lives. This is rampant in politics, media, and business today. Analyze your actions by thinking about how you spend your time and whom you spend it with. Pay attention to the crew you're hanging out with. We've all known those people who love to complain and just want to talk about how bad everything is— work, their bosses, their in-laws, neighbors, and so on. Are you participating in those kinds of negative conversations? Are you surrounded by people who have no ambition or drive? Do your day-to-day activities inspire you to seize the day—to work hard and succeed? Make a commitment to be in alignment by keeping your eye on your goal.

Thy Will Be Done

It's not uncommon to want something desperately in your life but face huge disappointment when you don't get it. You might feel that this loss permeates your life, but then something happens and you realize it all ultimately worked in your favor. One notable instance stands out for me: I grew up in Stillwater, Oklahoma, idolizing and playing alongside some of the best golfers in the world, among them Scott Verplank, Willie Wood, and Bob Tway, all of whom were members of the Cowboy national championship golf team at Oklahoma State. It was my dream to play golf there as well. I had some natural talent and a relentless work ethic, but I just wasn't good enough to be part of that team. Accepting this reality, I headed north to the University of Kansas, where I went from a walk-on to eventually becoming one of the top players and good enough to beat a few of those cowboys along the way. This was the direction my life needed to go for me to find success and fulfillment as a golfer. More importantly, it's where I met my beautiful wife, Jacqy. "Thy will be done," my mother repeatedly told me when I was growing up. Thy will be done indeed—just not always the way you think it will be.

It's important to remember that connecting with

your quintessence is a lifelong process and that detours don't mean you're veering away from your goal. Targets often need to be adjusted as life throws challenges in your path. But your end game should always remain stable and determined. As I said earlier, this line of effort is "front-loaded" and isn't easy, but not only does exploring your quintessence keep you on the path to living a more meaningful life, it becomes the foundation upon which CAVU is built—the framework for your next line of effort.

When I am aligned with my quintessence, I am

- a husband who strives to be the ultimate support system for my partner, who has had to shoulder the burden of being a military wife;

- a father who raises daughters to be confident, self-reliant, and service-driven;

- a fighter pilot whose experience in the military has guided me to bring attention to the fact that there's a need for education among military families;

- a PGA Professional who uses his gift to connect with others to help make my vision of providing scholarships to military families a reality;

- a speaker who shares openly my struggles and code of living to help others and uses the pulpit God has given me to connect with people and share my faith.

You too can use affirmative language to set your intentions and create your own declarations of quintessence. Try it now and refer to them as necessary.

3
Synchronicity

Just one week from the end of my second tour of duty in Iraq, I would fly one of the most demanding missions of my career. I found myself preparing to take off into a massive dust storm that was blowing across Iraq and the ground battle raging below me. This would mean a long night. I would be leading Brave flight, a two-ship formation that was fragged with six different air tasking orders (ATOs). In short, I'd be supporting six different missions, sitting in the cockpit for ten hours with no reprieve.

Before walking over to Life Support to begin my preparations, I swung by the flight kitchen and grabbed a couple of peanut butter and jelly sandwiches, a few bottles of water, and a packet of gummy worms.

Life Support looks a lot like an NFL locker room and contains the important equipment we use to stay alive while flying and in case we have to eject. Our names adorn our individual lockers and our gear hangs neatly, waiting for us to grab it in high pursuit. My first order of business there was focusing the diopter on my NVGs (night-vision goggles) so they perfectly aligned with my eyes' focus. Next I grabbed my G-suit and harness. The zippers on my G-suit easily slid up as the result of the ten pounds I had lost in the desert. The last thing I needed on the way out were piddle packs. I can affirm that the question "How do you go to the bathroom in an F-16?" is a very popular one asked of fighter pilots. Now you know the answer.

We stepped to the jet thirty minutes before launch. I saluted and shook hands with my crew chief and then reviewed the forms to ensure the jet was ready to fly. It always was, but redundancy is key. We trust our lives with the crew chief, but it's the pilot's ultimate decision whether or not to fly the jet.

The F-16's normally sleek body was dressed for *work* that night, bulked up by four 500-pound bombs and the Litening AT pod. Our loadout included two

GBU-38 JDAMs,* two GBU-12 laser-guided bombs, and 510 rounds of 20mm bullets. My preflight confirmed that all bombs were secure and properly carted.

With the walkaround completed, I climbed the ladder up to the cockpit. Strapped in the jet ten minutes before engine start, I had time to say a few prayers and to organize my cockpit. The Viper is not designed to have room for all of the stuff we need when we fly combat, and there's an art form to how every pilot sets himself up. We've been known to compare the setups of our jets to Burger King's motto—*Have it your way*—with each pilot possessing his or her own preferred method. It's crucial that everything is easily accessible, because anything you need will be reached for while simultaneously flying a jet in a very small altitude block at 350-plus knots.

I attached knee boards with Velcro leg straps on both thighs, which contained my lineup cards and blank 9-line forms. The 9-line is the standard format we use to work with the troops on the ground. On

---

* The Joint Direct Attack Munition (JDAM) is a guidance kit that converts unguided bombs, or "dumb bombs," into all-weather precision-guided munitions.

my left sat my bag full of various mission materials, including my "smart pack." On my right I stashed my NVGs, food, water, and my go-pills—Dexedrine—which is legally prescribed to fighter pilots because it helps keep our minds operating at the highest levels on long, intense missions.

I reached back to double-check that my smart pack was in the correct place. The smart pack is a small three-ring binder that contains the information I'll use to locate radio frequencies, grids, weapon data, and systems data. I think of it as my instructions for lethality.

Done. I turned on the light that was Velcroed to the side of my helmet. This little $20 gadget is a Godsend in my $30 million jet because it provides a powerful light that tracks my head movements and allows me to read the immense amount of information in my smart pack.

Brave 22 cleared for takeoff.

Moments after getting clearance, my wingman and I blasted into the pitch black, with no visual reference as to what was up or down. I was tempted to put on my NVGs, but I knew it wasn't safe to use them until I had climbed 1,000 feet into the sky. I am religious about my flow and habit patterns, because things in the F-16 can go wrong very quickly, and putting NVGs on too early can cause a loss of spatial orientation. In 2007, the community lost a great fighter pilot, Major Kevin Sonnenberg, on takeoff due to a suspected early donning of his NVGs. His jet went into a slow roll and quickly became unrecoverable.

Once I was safely airborne, my NVGs went on and the world transformed into light green. Though my depth perception was almost zero and my field of view was narrowed to the width of a soda straw, NVGs contain amazing technology that allows one to see a cigarette burning from thirty miles away. No joke.

The airspace over Iraq was the busiest, most concentrated in the world, and that night it felt more populated than any other night. Our F-16s were flying in one layer of the sky, but we were stacked with flying assets from every branch of the military—Apache and Black Hawk helicopters, Navy F-18s, AWACS air traffic control planes, J-STARS and U2 intelligence planes, and various unmanned platforms, like the Predator drone. Each of us brings a different LOE to the fight, but the Viper is the pointy end of the spear—the one that is most often called to support the heroes on the ground.

But we're not without our own support. "Kingpin" is the call sign of the one hyper-smart dude whom we rely on and who runs Operation Iraqi Freedom over the radios. He, in turn, is backed up by many support assets in the Combined Air Operations Center (CAOC), and it is he who deals out the orders quickly and precisely. It's not uncommon to start a mission with one tasking in mind, only to be immediately redirected by King-pin. If a situation arises and our troops on the ground need help, we are re-rolled to support them. Flexibility is the key to airpower, and a mindset that can handle sudden change is mandatory for a fighter pilot.

Scott "Rookie" Rooks, my wingman, was in a two-mile radar trail behind me. Scott and I are the best of friends and we spend a lot of time together back in Oklahoma. Rookie is also a scratch golfer, and we had a running joke that we had the lowest combined handicap over Iraq. Our time together in Tulsa couldn't be more different than what we faced in the hostile skies tonight. A typical day back there included eighteen holes, followed by a nice steak and a few glasses of red wine on his back deck. In Iraq it was all business: We were flying our F-16s in the hottest combat zone in the world over 88AS, the grid that encompassed most of Baghdad.

Suddenly, Kingpin interrupted with a pressing situation. We received notification that our tasking order was changing. Troops in contact (TIC)—Army and Marine forces fighting in close proximity to the enemy—needed our immediate support. Getting re-rolled to our new location was the equivalent of working a four-dimensional puzzle, one that needed to be solved urgently. I consulted my smart pack and punched in frequencies and coordinates in the up-front control to get the location of the TIC. I pushed the throttle up and the F-16 responded with raw power . . . a feeling that never gets old. I watched my fuel gauge spin over my right knee and noticed that I was going to need some gas soon. I set a new joker . . . *bingo.*★ At the speed I was flying, executing this task was like playing a video game (except obviously no one fighting a war gets three lives).

Flying just below the speed of sound, we arrived at our location within minutes.

Brave 22 push Blue 41.

We checked in with JTAC, or joint terminal attack controller. JTAC is embedded with the ground forces and is specially trained to communicate directly with pilots. If the situation on the ground dictates airstrikes, he has the authority to call it in. JTAC owns the ord-

---

★ *Bingo* refers to how much fuel is required to get back to base, and *joker* is how much is needed before any maneuvering should be terminated. When a mission changes, so do the fuel requirements—new joker/bingo.

nance on our fully loaded jets. As I received an abbreviated 9-line over the radio, I could hear the chilling sounds of war in the background—the clashing of bullets ricocheting off his Humvee. The JTAC's voice remained calm as he keyed the mike despite troops fighting for their lives. Even though I was 25,000 feet above the fight, I could feel how emotionally charged the situation was. Though I was nervous, my pulse remained steady, a skill I have refined in the jet but first learned while playing competitive golf.

The JTAC called for an immediate show of force, which is the fastest way to eliminate the threat. He cleared us to 500 feet off the deck. I elevatored the jet down through the weather deck to the low block and made a high-speed pass with my afterburner while kicking out flares that lit up the night sky. To anyone below, this sound was deafening, and the sheer power of the F-16 literally shook the ground. It proved the perfect remedy when the insurgents disengaged. Our work was done (temporarily), and I let JTAC know we'd be around all night if he needed us.

My gas was getting uncomfortably low, which meant we'd require some quick help from our tanker brothers. Thankfully, the request I'd made on the way to TIC earlier was granted, and Kingpin had moved the "Texaco in the sky" forward to where we were located.

Sometimes the F-16 flies to the tankers, but there are times, like this one, when the fuel has to come to us. As you might imagine, refueling in midair at night requires coordination, precision, and concentration.

Kingpin . . . Brave, snap 185 for 15—tankers at FL210.

I turned my jet south and used my radar to lock on the KC-135 and run the intercept. Rolling out in a one-mile trail, I cleared my wingman to the left wing of the tanker. Peering through my NVGs, I saw that the boom was extended. This was my comm-out signal that I was cleared to the pre-contact position. *Cool.* I slowly pulled up to the back of the tanker, carefully monitoring my closure in the head-up display (HUD) to ensure I didn't overrun them. I opened my air fueling door on the spine of the jet and tucked under the huge KC-135. Lights on the belly of the tanker guided me into position, and I heard a familiar *clunk* as we connected. For the next ten minutes we both flew at precisely 310 knots (356 miles per hour) as I fueled up.

Wiggle your fingers and toes, I thought.

This is a technique I learned back at Luke to relax while I make constant small corrections for pitch and power to stay connected to the tanker. After about ten minutes I felt the pressure disconnect and saw my air refuel light blink. A quick glance down over my right knee showed the tanks were full and feeding. I gave a salute to the boomer and a quick "strength and honor" on the radio, and after Rookie gassed up we got right back into the fight.

By the time we finished our mission taskings for the night, Rookie and I were cooked. We had been in the air for over eight hours, supporting multiple taskings, which required us to refuel in midair five times. It was grueling, and yet we still had another hour of flying ahead of us before we made it back to base.

Brave flight fence out.

With that sign we could finally safe up our weapons and set our cockpit switches from combat mode to navigation mode. The last few hours had been a helmet fire. "Helmet fire" is a phrase unique to the fighter-pilot community, but one that almost anyone can understand: It describes the moment when one's brain is overloaded with more information than it can process. We rendezvoused with our tanker buddies for one last sip of gas as we pressed south out of Iraq down the Persian Gulf and headed back to base.

The universe has more mysterious methods, though. As we passed into Kuwaiti airspace, Rookie came over the interflight UHF radio and made an unusual request.

"Hey, Noonan, turn down your lights," he said.

"Turn down my lights?" I asked, still trying to decompress from the night's mission.

"Your interior lights," he said. "Turn them down."

With the autopilot engaged, I reached over my right leg and turned the dials counterclockwise. The green glow gradually faded in the cockpit until I was engulfed in blackness.

"Okay," I responded, still wondering why he had told me to do so.

But then came his answer. "Look up," Rookie said.

In the fog of war, my mind hadn't processed that a cold front had swept away the dust storm and that what was left behind was incredible to see. Instead of the usual carnage of war, I looked through the unrestricted view of the F-16 bubble canopy at the most explosive natural display of light I have ever seen in my life. The sky was awash in infinite blue space, dotted with stars that sparkled with brilliant light. It no longer looked like a war zone in the Middle East but somewhere infinitely peaceful. Perched on the forward edge of the jet at 31,000 feet, I sat in awe of the millions of stars putting on a personal show for us. As the show progressed, the stars resembling their own singular blinking worlds, I asked myself how it was possible to have gone from complete chaos to a place of pure calm so quickly. My only explanation? That this wasn't a random or chance encounter, but rather a divine and spiritual force. It was my first encounter with the power of synchronicity, and I would never look at the world the same.

LOE #2: SYNCHRONICITY

Synchronicity, or what I like to call "chance with purpose," is how God connects moments in our lives. It's an omnipresent current that links you to the universe and guides your intended path, the force that connects you to people and to other meaningful experiences. Moments of synchronicity are signs from God.

The concept of synchronicity was coined by the pioneering psychologist Carl Jung, who spoke of some events as "meaningful coincidences." I believe synchronicity is much deeper than simple coincidence. Meeting your spouse at a party you almost didn't attend, talking to someone in line at a coffee shop and learning they work at the company where you've just had an interview, or looking up just in time to avoid a car accident are all examples of synchronicity. It's someone on your mind who pops onto your caller ID, or that you stumbled upon *Fly Into the Wind* and are now reading it.

The synchronicity I experienced in combat when I turned down my lights to reveal that heavenly display was a reminder that if I didn't pay attention, I was going to miss out on powerful God moments both big and small. Life is synchronized beyond human comprehension, and it has potential to bring life-changing results, but here's the secret: You can tap into it. I have broken down synchronicity into two primary types below.

Type 1: Game Changers

This type of synchronicity provides a vector that alters your path and leads you in a new direction. These are big, life-altering moments.

Extraordinary events are often the result of game-changing synchronicity, of being at the right place at the right time and *being observant* of the amazing possibilities therein. Game-changing synchronicity occurred, for example, in Scotland in the 1920s when Dr. Alexander Fleming, a bacteriologist at St. Mary's Hospital in London, returned from vacation and noticed that mold had contaminated his Petri dishes. The mold that infiltrated the Petri dish, *Penicillium notatum,* seemed to have stopped *Staphylococcus* from growing as it normally would. Could mold be inhibiting the growth of bacteria? Fleming wondered. He knew this could lead to a massive improvement in mortality rates, so he performed more tests to confirm his theory. While there was much work to be done to develop penicillin as we know it today, fourteen years later the first patient was saved from a deadly infection in the United States. Since that discovery, millions of lives have been saved thanks to Dr. Fleming's game-changing moment of synchronicity and his observant instincts.

We can point to another example years later, this time on the other side of the pond. George Herbert Walker Bush secured a rich legacy as one of the youngest aviators to fly during World War II, as a congressman and the tenth U.S. ambassador to the United Nations, as director of the CIA, then vice president under Ronald Reagan, and eventually the forty-first president of the United States. However, his legacy would not be celebrated if it wasn't for an incredible moment of game-changing synchronicity. Shortly after Bush was promoted to lieutenant junior grade, he piloted a Grumman TBM Avenger aircraft that attacked the Japanese on an island called Chichijima during World War II. Bush and three other Avengers faced intense fire. Bush's plane was hit, and his engine was immediately set ablaze. Still, he was able to release his bombs over his target and make several hits before flying miles away from the island, where he and his crew member jumped out of the burning aircraft. His crew member's parachute did not open, and Bush was left alone in hostile open waters, floating in his raft. In a game-changing moment of synchronicity, a nearby U.S. submarine rescued him. Had that vessel not been nearby, he likely would have been captured by enemy forces. Bush's list of accomplishments as president is long, but a few notable contributions include playing a key role in the ending of the Cold War, liberating Kuwait, passing the Americans with Disabilities Act, and creating the Points of Light initiative, the largest organization dedicated to volunteer service. Without that key moment of synchronicity, our nation's history would look very different than it does today.

Type 2: Fluid

Fluid synchronicity is the affirmation that you are on the right path and the encouragement to stay the course. Fluid synchronicity consists of those signs that are meaningful to you and that consistently appear in your life. Moments of fluid synchronicity may include seeing a number or name repeated with frequency, encountering the same symbol regularly, thinking about something and then having it happen, or an interaction with someone who will play a role in your journey.

Ever since that day on the golf course when I realized that the origins of 13 were rooted in *new beginnings,* the number 13 has brought fluid synchronicity into my life. I felt a renewed conviction for my destined path. I began to understand that HE (13) is everywhere. Suddenly I found my Avis spot flashing space B13, or my flying out of gate 1367 (double 13s—6 + 7 = 13). I can't tell you how many times my bill at a restaurant has added up to 13, the gas pump has stopped on 13 gallons, or my wife has called my cell at 1313 hours. I know that when the 13th day of every month pops up on the calendar, it will be a day full of blessings. When I am faced with difficult decisions or a professional or personal roadblock, the appearance of 13 serves as a reminder from God that I'm on the correct course. While the number 13 remains my most consistent form of fluid synchronicity, I also get a boost every time I encounter a random coin on the street; they are like breadcrumbs from God. I smile whenever I read the phrase "In God We Trust" on every coin.

Fluid synchronicity is by no means limited to numbers (or coins). Fluid synchronicity arrives in the form of any small but significant reminder to you. This could include symbols, patterns, phrases, songs—anything that captures your attention and serves as a confirmation from your higher power that you're on the right path.

While that beautiful display of starlight opened my eyes to the concept of synchronicity, it was the number

13 that inspired me to become a "watcher." Most of us move through the day not noticing much of what's going on around us. At work or in school, we focus on what needs to get done or on events that directly impact us at that moment. I get it, this is a big part of life. But being a watcher—in a position to actually notice and experience moments of synchronicity—requires us to be less self-centric and function as active participants throughout our days. As you begin work on this line of effort, it can be difficult to know what to watch for, and it is easy to overthink and to look so intently for signs that you'll potentially miss the small moments of synchronicity that are meant for you. To help narrow your focus about what to watch for, try the following:

- Take an inventory of different areas in your life. Note if you can connect the dots between any of them. For example, be aware if there is something grabbing your attention at work, at home, in your neighborhood. A number, a color, a sound.

- Practice listening to your intuition. Open your senses to become aware of patterns, numbers, or symbols that are making themselves known.

Don't ignore them; they are popping up for a reason.

- There's no judgment about what speaks to you and what you choose to watch for. Everything has meaning if it is important to you, which means that meaning is also personal. Only you can decide what you want to watch for.

- It's hard to notice what's happening in your immediate environment if you are constantly looking at your phone. Give yourself permission to disconnect from the distractions and devices for a certain period of time each day and see if it makes a difference.

Accumulating moments of game-changing and fluid synchronicity will draw you one crucial step closer to achieving CAVU, but to benefit from everything it has to offer, you must regard these moments as invitations from God to make a change, take a risk, or make a concrete decision to pursue essential goals. Have the courage to use reckless faith when God calls to you through a moment of synchronicity and see where it can take you.

4
Volition

During the fall semester of my junior year at Kansas, I signed up for a class called "Sports Psychology 101." As a golfer, I was intrigued by the concept and thought maybe the class would better help me execute under pressure. Stress is every golfer's enemy: In golf, like many different areas of life, true power comes from a place of calm. But if I'm being completely honest, I also thought "Sports Psychology 101" would be the easiest class I took that semester.

Pushing through the big wooden doors that led into the classroom, I was happy to see so many other athletes; I guess we all had the same idea—an easy A. On the first day of class, I found a seat and waited for the professor to arrive, but as the seconds turned to minutes, the other students grew restless and the chatter grew more pronounced. Some of the football players even started tossing a ball back and forth to pass the time.

Finally, a good-looking young professor wearing a polo shirt and khakis entered and walked straight to the front of the room. He didn't say a word, not even turning around to introduce himself. He wrote on the whiteboard in big, bold letters:

VOLITION

The professor stood there quietly, waiting for the class to settle down. When the room was finally quiet, and he was confident he had our attention, he finally spoke. "Does anyone know what 'volition' means?" he asked. The students glanced blankly back and forth at each other. Similarly, I hadn't seen that word before and had no idea what it meant.

"Volition is the most powerful word in the world," he continued. "It's the power of choice. Every day you are free to choose. You can make a positive choice or a negative choice. You can choose to have grit, to be uncommon. You can choose to follow your heart and pursue your dreams. Understand that your choices, whatever they may be, will culminate to write the legacy of your life. Do not waste this gift."

I left that classroom galvanized by the idea of volition, the concept that *I,* and I alone, had the power to make choices. That I could wake up every morning and determine the course of my day was a small revelation, sure, but what if I could round up all these choices to better shape my legacy?

Later that afternoon, excited by what I had learned in class, I decided to tell my teammates that I was going to turn my dream of becoming a fighter pilot into a reality. They all laughed at me. At that point in my life, people typically responded unenthusiastically to my dream of becoming a golf professional and a fighter pilot. They seemed to relish telling me that it was unreasonable and unattainable. But what I learned in that lecture was a gift that blinded me to the negative comments (or doubts or eye rolls or laughter). Instead, I was guided by my determination, desire, and commitment to a big idea. I understood that it was my choice to follow this dream, whether or not the world deemed it realistic. Volition would be the fuel to help get me where I needed to be.

LOE #3: *VOLITION*

Volition, or the exercising of one's will, is the most powerful tool human beings have. On the surface, volition is about choosing to pursue something with every ounce of energy. You may be thinking—and quite correctly—why *wouldn't* one pursue something desirable with every ounce of energy? Why would one make choices that don't fully support a big vision for oneself? But engaging our volition isn't always easy because, at its core, it's about something much deeper than just making a choice. It's about making an *absolute commitment* to a code of living. Every single choice you make follows a logical progression:

- I won't
- I can't
- I'd like to
- I'll try
- I can
- I will

The path from "I won't" to "I will" is a treacherous one marked by obstacles and doubts, and as you're moving along it's possible that your end goal won't be in sight for a very long time. But it's crucial to keep forging on. The commitment to "I will" means a pledge to stay on that path no matter what, to open yourself up to all of the joys, challenges, and unexpected surprises that are part of your ascent to greatness.

The power of volition has shaped our world. It's this force that kept Rosa Parks in her seat on that bus in Montgomery, Alabama, in 1955. When Rosa Parks reflected on that incident nearly forty years later, it's as if she pinpointed the exact moment her volition was ignited: "When that white driver stepped back toward us, when he waved his hand and ordered us up and out of our seats, I felt a determination cover my body like a quilt on a winter night," she said. Parks's activation of her volition set off a series of events that would change our nation forever. Her arrest provoked massive bus boycotts that played a crucial role in the ever-important quest for civil rights.

Negative Choices and Doubts Are Integral to the Plan

It's no question that Christianity has formed the foundation of *my* volition. But also taken as a moral tale, the Bible story of Peter elegantly demonstrates how both positive and negative choices play roles in directing (and diverting) us along the path to our goal.

Peter, one of Jesus's twelve apostles, is a relatable and sympathetic figure: His actions can be hasty and rash, maybe even reckless, but they consistently stem from passion, which is the fuel that drives our volition. This simplified story about him demonstrates the arc that volition takes:

Peter is in a boat with the other disciples while Jesus is off in the distance, praying by himself. While they're waiting for Jesus to return to the boat, the winds and waves kick up fiercely. The boat is tossed back and forth in the storm and the disciples are afraid, anxious for Jesus to come back. Suddenly, they see a ghostlike figure moving toward them on the water, which causes them to become even more frightened. Jesus calls out to them, telling them not to be afraid. But that isn't good enough for Peter, who wants to know if it's really Jesus; and unlike the other disciples he's willing to take action to get the answer. Peter shouts out something along the lines of, "If that's really you walking on the water, prove it! Call me to walk on the water too." He hops off the boat and actually walks on the water toward Jesus, but soon becomes distracted by the fact that he is walking on water in the middle of a storm. As the winds get stronger and the waves bigger, Peter becomes afraid and cries out to Jesus. Jesus extends his hand to him and says, "O you of little faith, why did you doubt?"

Using volition can be a frightening experience at first. Some of the biggest decisions of my life, such as joining the Air Force, starting Folds of Honor, and building The Patriot Golf Club, were gut decisions. Like Peter's walk on the water, those decisions were accompanied by huge moments of doubt and anxiety, but the more doubt I embraced, the more passionate my resolve became.

The tale in Matthew 8:23–27 isn't the only time Peter employs volition; the story of the Last Supper demonstrates his radical determination as well. In the hours following the Last Supper, Peter falls victim to fear and weakness, denying three times that he knows Jesus. Being known in the Bible solely as a person who denies knowing Jesus could be the end of Peter's story, but it's not. Recognizing his own failure, Peter demonstrates great humility and resilience by having the courage to right his wrong. When Jesus is on the cross, the other apostles hide in fear, not wanting to see their savior suffer, but Peter doesn't. He appears before Jesus at the crucifixion and then is the first apostle to go to his tomb upon his death. After the resurrection, Jesus offers his forgiveness to Peter. By forgiving Peter, Jesus restores him to the ministry, making it clear that he is still part of God's plan. Peter is chosen by Jesus as the *Rock* upon which the Christian church is built, and he goes on to preach the gospel for the rest of his life.

Fear and weakness make us prone to making some bad choices, but Peter's story shows us that the greater the fall, the greater the opportunity to rise. Volition provides *options*. You may feel stuck in life, in the midst of a dark period, or may just be struggling to stay focused on your goals, but volition is the tool that can elevate you to a better place. If you're down, you are by no means out. Find your "I will" and use volition to get up again.

Are You a Victim of Common Assumption?

Assumptions, or accepting societal norms, can keep you locked in a mental prison. When you think about your larger goals, don't let common assumptions keep you from getting to the final stage of "I will." Common assumptions run rampant, from convincing yourself that you're not up to the task to comparing your efforts to those of others around you.

Some of the greatest examples of volition require an

unwavering commitment to "I will" in order to break down society's common assumptions. When you tune in to Fox Sports to watch NASCAR, one thing you won't see is that every Sunday starts with a drivers' chapel service. At the Folds of Honor QT 500, the Atlanta Motor Speedway asked me to share my story during chapel with the drivers, during which time I met the fastest female driver on earth, Danica Patrick. I had always been a fan of her no-barriers spirit but would be blessed with the opportunity to get to know her outside of her race world. Danica's story is all about having the courage and faith that she could go faster than anyone in the world. "I was brought up to be the fastest driver, not the fastest girl," Patrick has said of her talents. Her reckless faith gave her the confidence to drop out of high school and move to England to pursue her dream of becoming a race car driver. It was there where she signed to drive with Rahal Letterman Lanigan Racing and became the first woman to win a race on the IndyCar Circuit. Danica would leave IndyCar to pursue NASCAR and continue to have great success on and off the track. She was named one of *Time*'s "100 Most Influential People" and has appeared in a record-setting fourteen Super Bowl commercials.

I believe that each and every one of us has the power within ourselves to create the life that we really want. And I want to inspire you to conquer your dreams, both professionally and personally.

—Danica Patrick

The NFL contains numerous examples of the power of volition. If not for it, we would never have heard of Tom Brady or Richard Sherman, two legends among the many who were once lowly draft picks. In fact, the NFL's undrafted players, who have been deemed by the experts as statistical throwaways, have more players on NFL rosters (481) than first- and second-round picks combined (480).

I have also been a prisoner of common assumption, long after I thought that was even possible. After being blessed with a thriving career that included becoming an F-16 fighter pilot, a PGA Professional, and the founder and CEO of Folds of Honor, I wanted to create something that would help spread the life-changing power of volition. It was my goal to start an apparel line that inspired people to go out into the world and make positive choices, a uniform for *life*, if you will. In our initial meetings about Volition America with folks in the apparel industry, I was presented with dozens of reasons as to why it would never work. I knew nothing

about the clothing industry, and these people had decades of combined experience, so it was tempting to let
their doubts dash my dream. But as I started to process
what was said at the meetings—any design obstacles or
the fact that manufacturing and distribution costs were
too big—I started to wonder if I was just a victim of the
expectations society, or more pointedly this industry,
places upon success. Was it simply assumed by most
people that these particular challenges would make it
impossible for us to succeed?

Of course, I never expected it to be easy. There
would be countless obstacles, but once I saw that common assumption was holding me back, I was more
determined to stay the course. Similarly, if you're facing pushback on your journey, or find yourself riddled
with self-doubt, assess whether common assumption is
holding you back and then attempt the following:

- Determine: Is this a real problem that needs to
  be solved, or are you assuming it's a problem
  with no facts to back that up?

- If it is a random assumption, challenge it. Why
  are you drawing this conclusion? What thoughts
  are running through your head that lead you to
  believe it? If it is a real problem, take time to

consider the issues. Are the obstacles really so unreasonable? How can you break them down and make them more accessible?

It's crucial to harness your passion and determination when pursuing a dream, because there will be plenty of people along the way who will be quick to tell you why it's not possible. The experts and their "you can't do that" attitudes fuel me in the deepest way. I am honored to say that Volition America is now a successful line of golf apparel made in partnership with Puma. Our *uniform for life* received incredible attention after Gary Woodland won the U.S. Open in 2019 wearing Volition America. Gary and I go way back; I first met him when he transferred to the University of Kansas (he had played college basketball before transitioning to golf). I am nine years older than him, but golf was the impetus for our connection, and one of the reasons why we have become closer over the years. When Gary got his PGA Tour card, he called me to share the news, and I still remember the excitement in his voice.

"Dan, I'd like to put Folds of Honor on my tour bag," he told me.

It's a big deal when a golfer decides to embrace a brand by displaying its logo on his bag, and at that point his career really started to take off. Gary was winning tournaments, and I was proud every time I saw him out there living his dream. I always knew he was a phenomenal golfer, but to watch one of your closest friends pour in a putt on the eighteenth hole to finish thirteen under par and win the U.S. Open (there's that number again!) is miraculous, a game-changing moment of synchronicity and confirmation that every bit of resistance I faced creating Folds of Honor and Volition America was just part of this journey to something bigger and better. Not long ago, I was building Folds above my garage and struggling to start a clothing line that would empower people with volition. Now one of the world's greatest golfers was boasting the Volition logo on his shirt and displaying Folds of Honor on his bag.

I love that Gary wears Volition America when he plays, because *volition* speaks to who he is as a person. After winning the U.S. Open, Gary made the usual media circuit to all the big television shows, but he chose to make it more about the power of will than his own achievements. Sitting right by his side during some of his interviews was Amy Bockerstette, a twenty-year-old student with Down syndrome who had landed a golf scholarship at Paradise Valley Community College in Phoenix. After participating in the 2018 Waste Management Open (Gary was defending champion), he invited Amy to play the sixteenth hole with him. With thousands watching, Gary teed up the ball for Amy, who hit a solid shot but landed it in the greenside bunker. Gary didn't want her to get nervous trying to make a shot and offered to help. She turned to him and said, "I got this." She perfectly nailed the next shot and made the putt for a par! Gary felt that this moment had inspired him on a life-changing level, and instead of basking in the glory of winning a major golf tournament, he chose to make it about something bigger—a young woman's extraordinary achievement.

Volition can create a never-ending loop of positivity. While it was awesome to have Gary compete with a Volition shirt on his back, his encounter with Amy is something I will never forget. Amy's path to playing golf couldn't have looked more different from Gary's. Gary played sports his entire life, while Amy has had to tackle enormous physical challenges to play the sport. Though she had natural talent, her disability made things more challenging. Her low muscle tone meant that she got worn out easily, and if she wasn't careful, she'd become dehydrated and get sick. Her parents didn't know if she'd have the stamina to last eighteen holes. To get her through, they created an energy management plan, monitoring her health and fueling her with water and energy drinks during tournaments. Despite her talent, it is still not easy for Amy to make it through a tournament, and yet she does it with determination and a big smile on her face. Volition is a huge part of what gets her going, and to this day she's quick to point out (as she did with Gary during that round) that she doesn't need a pro golfer to get her out of a tight spot; *she's got it.* Volition can be contagious, as demonstrated by the millions of people who have been moved by Amy's extraordinary example that our choices have the power to keep us going even when things are tough.

Volition is the fuel that empowers you to achieve CAVU. The world is full of noise and excuses, but armed with the power of volition you can break through it to become anything and to change anything. Your choices will culminate to write the legacy of your life. Just make it a legacy you're proud of.

5

Parasitic Drag

Pushing the F-16 up over the satin-blue waters of the Pacific Ocean, I could feel its power coursing through my veins. We were "fighting" against jets from the Hawaii Air National Guard (HIANG), and I sat snugly in my single-seat Viper, ready to lead a four-ship formation of "red air"* in replicating Russian tactics to challenge the blue-air F-15 Eagles. Our air-to-air training is much more challenging than anything we will likely ever face in combat. These days we're highly unlikely to engage in air-to-air combat, but we always remain proficient.

---

* The term refers to any entity that America could potentially fight.

Fight's on came over the common frequency, signaling the beginning of the training exercise. As I drove east with the sun at my back, I recalled the phrase "Lose sight, lose fight," one of the oldest and most effective tactics for fighter pilots. Basically, if the enemy can't see us coming, we're at an obvious advantage. This tactic was used regularly in combat through the Vietnam War, but fortunately for my generation of fighter pilots, there are advanced radars and air-to-air missiles that give us an advantage well beyond hiding in the sun. We also have a HUD that works in tandem with a Boeing Joint Helmet Mounted Cueing System (JHMCS). The JHMCS combines a magnetic head tracker with a display that projects data onto the visor. The device does this by synchronizing the aircraft sensors with my movements, so that all data appears over my right eye, no matter which direction I'm looking. This also enables me to aim sensors and weapons; wherever I look, the weapons follow. We call it *look kill.*

As I led the formation, *Mach 1.2* displayed on my HUD. I might have been simulating a deadly battle, but I couldn't help but smile. Crossing into the realm of supersonic never gets old. The truth is, the actual sensation of breaking the sound barrier is subtle. If you're really paying attention, you'll feel a slight bump in the air, but the only way you know you're super is that little green number in the HUD. Every time I break through Mach 1, I give a mental salute to Chuck Yeager. I know how much effort and sacrifice went into making this feat possible.

Chuck Yeager was a combat fighter pilot during World War II who flew sixty-four missions over Europe. He shot down thirteen German planes—five in a single day—which earned him the incredible distinction of "ace in a day." He was eventually shot down over France, but the French underground helped him avoid capture. After the war, Yeager volunteered to fly the experimental X-1 rocket plane, built by Bell Aircraft Company to explore the possibility of supersonic flight. For years, aviators believed that man was not meant to fly faster than the speed of sound, the pervading theory holding that something called "parasitic transonic drag rise" would tear apart any aircraft. *Drag* refers to the forces that oppose the motion of an object through the air, and *parasitic drag* is defined as any drag that isn't connected to the production of lift.

The early flights of X-1 ran into problems. As the jet approached Mach 1, it suffered from violent vibrations and became unresponsive. At Mach 1, the air in front of an aircraft compresses to the point where it becomes virtually a solid wall. As you can imagine, flying the world's fastest plane into a "wall" seemed unwise to say the least, and for some time the theory of its impossibility held.

Chuck Yeager wasn't convinced, though, nor was his friend and colleague engineer Jack Ridley. The flight engineer on the X-1 program, Ridley was certain that they could break the sound barrier with the engineering modifications he had made to the tail of the X-1 plane. After a third attempt, when Yeager nearly lost control of the plane, another crew member had suggested that the X-1's horizontal tail should be shifted just slightly. Yeager was willing to put his life in Ridley's hands once again if it meant being the first man to break the sound barrier and proving the scientists wrong. He was clutching on to the hope that his rocket-powered vehicle would defy the laws of physics (as they were understood in 1946) and break the barrier rather than shaking apart and exploding with Yeager inside it.

As a decorated combat pilot and a top test pilot, Yeager had been hand-selected for this secret mission by top brass, who had a lot of faith in him. But on the day of his flight, that faith might have been eroded if they saw the crude instrument that accompanied him inside the cockpit. A couple of days earlier, Yeager had fallen off of a horse and broken two ribs, but, not wanting to miss out on the opportunity of flying the mission, he kept his injury secret by avoiding going to a doctor on the base, seeking medical treatment off base instead. He was in so much pain that he was unable to reach out to close the door of the cockpit. Just moments before the soon-to-be historic flight, Ridley found a wooden broom handle and haphazardly crafted a device Yeager could use to shut the door. Needless to say, this was *not* standard equipment.

The mission could not have been more dangerous. A pilot whose injuries technically rendered him unfit for flying was going to pilot a rocket (and a rocket is really just a controlled explosion) up against a barrier of solid air—without anyone knowing for sure if it was going to work. But on October 14, 1947, Yeager successfully flew the X-1 *Glamorous Glennis* (named for his wife) over Rogers Dry Lake in Southern California. The X-1 was lifted to an altitude of 25,000 feet by a B-29 aircraft and then released from the bomb bay in the underbelly of the plane, rocketing to 40,000 feet and exceeding 662 miles per hour (the sound barrier at that altitude). Ridley's tail design worked, and the horizontal stabilizer successfully eliminated enough parasitic drag that Yeager was able to finally fly faster than the speed of sound.

LOE #4: ELIMINATE PARASITIC DRAG

Yeager and Ridley were committed to breaking through the sound barrier, but it wasn't until Ridley figured out how to take parasitic drag out of the equation that this monumental aeronautic feat was accomplished. This LOE is focused on getting rid of stuff that prevents you from breaking through barriers to get to where you want to be. If you want to experience CAVU, you must eliminate the parasitic drag in your life. It manifests itself in many forms, but make no mistake: Any form of parasitic drag you carry can prevent you from having healthy relationships, a successful career, pursuing your dreams, or being your best self.

There are two evolutions within this LOE. The first is to identify any parasitic drag in your life, and the second is to replace it with the "right stuff" to help you engineer a *high-speed, low-drag lifestyle.* If you get rid of something, you must replace it with something else. This remove-and-replace relationship is a critical step toward eliminating our unwanted behaviors for the long haul.

There is tremendous science behind breaking negative addictions outlined in Charles Duhigg's book *The Power of Habit.* Ironically, the inspiration for the seven-year study and subsequent book started in Iraq, with

Duhigg's fascination with the wit of a U.S. Army major in Kufa, Iraq, who nipped riots in the bud by persuading the small town's mayor to keep food vendors out of large and growing gatherings. When people couldn't fuel their anger and energy with kebabs, as they usually did, they just left. Remove the food, and you break the cycle of the habit.

Your drag is unique to you and your own life experiences, but I broke it down into four categories that represent some major sources of parasitic drag.

Drag #1: The Poisonous Mindsets—Emotions Such as Anger, Resentment, Bitterness, Grudges, Guilt, and Shame

The poisonous mindset sits at the top of the list because the emotions it harbors are an incredibly heavy burden to carry. If you possess any all-consuming emotions, know that they have the power to infect every part of your life. We've all felt wronged at times, or that life is unfair (and it often is). But if you allow those emotions to fester, you run the risk of marking your life with darkness, the complete opposite of CAVU.

Fortunately, there is an antidote available that can reset the poisonous mindset and position you for flight, and it's called forgiveness. Forgiveness requires being willing to release those emotions. It's an honest and forthcoming declaration to let them go. Forgiveness isn't necessarily about the physical act of apology; it's about going deeper to create an intentional commitment with yourself and God by letting go of what's holding you back. Forgive others and forgive yourself. It's understanding that we are all created in God's image, and as HE forgives us so must we forgive. If you don't forgive, whatever darkness you are harboring will always have power over you.

Reliving the moment in which I made that careless mistake with the landing gear on my jet created a lot of anxiety and caused some serious emotional scar tissue, but it was only when I chose to forgive *myself* that I was able to shed this parasitic drag from my life. I found I could only move forward when I focused on the positive contributions I had made in the F-16, the missions I had flown that I knew made America a safer place.

When it comes to searching for inner peace, forgiveness is a central tenet across all religions. In Catholicism, there's the sacrament of reconciliation, the idea that no matter what, your sins are forgiven in the eyes of God. The peace of mind this can bring is a beautiful thing. In Judaism, forgiveness is considered a mitzvah or divine command. The Torah actually forbids the taking of revenge or the bearing of grudges (Leviticus 19:18). In the Muslim faith, there are many different names used for God in the Quran, among them Al-Ghafoor (the Most Forgiving), Al-Afuw (the Pardoner), and Al-Tawwab (the Acceptor of Repentance). And in the Buddhist faith, the theme of forgiveness is perfectly distilled by this quote: "Holding on to anger is like grasping a hot coal with the intent of throwing it at someone else; you are the one who gets burned." My favorite words on forgiveness were spoken by Gandhi, perhaps the beacon of moral judgment: "The weak can never forgive. Forgiveness is the attribute of the strong." It's easy to focus on the differences between faiths, but the major takeaway they share is that there is simply no room for feelings of revenge, anger, or bitterness in a peaceful and healthy life.

Drag #2: Your Invisible Prison—Limiting Beliefs, Negative Circumstances, and Debilitating Relationships

It is very common to feel trapped by your personal, invisible prison and the million reasons why you can't get to the place you'd like to in life. Truth be told, the first day I walked into UPT, I was full of doubt as I looked around the room. I was a kid from Oklahoma who had gone to the University of Kansas and was now surrounded by chiseled-jawed, broad-shouldered grads of the Air Force Academy in blue dress uniforms. I was pulled down by limiting beliefs that I didn't belong and that the other wannabes were smarter and had been groomed more carefully than I had been. That night in my room, as I sat in quiet despondence, I realized that there was no way I could continue to fly alone. I started to pray. It was a much deeper kind of prayer than on a typical Sunday morning, and in this moment I felt a new connection in my conversation with God. I made a commitment to begin each day with thirty minutes of prayer. The challenges and demands of pilot training were still present—I still had to make it through the day—but I felt less alone and more prepared to take it all on. Prayer served as a form of solace and an amazing source of strength. From that day forward, I was renewed with a newfound understanding of the awesome power of prayer. God was my wingman.

We have all felt the negative impact of our desires, the overwhelming feeling of enormity as well as the temporary relief that comes from just "giving up." Equally unforgiving is the prospect of being surrounded by people who exhibit the same type of toxic, self-limiting behavior that you are prone to and who bring their drag directly into your life. You can't achieve your highest goals if you have built an inefficient environment that beats you back with negativity as you cross the threshold. To break out of your invisible prison for good, consider the following.

Connect to a Higher Power

As a Catholic, I engage in thirty minutes of prayer each morning, and I do my best to attend daily mass. I travel frequently for work, but it's easy to find a church to visit (and it's exciting to see different churches across the country). Going to mass only takes up about twenty minutes of my morning (yes, mass is much longer on Sundays), but its impact on me has been phenomenal. Attending mass and practicing prayer helps me channel gratitude, gives me the strength to face challenges and be open to new possibilities, and, most significantly, reminds me that I am not alone.

You certainly don't have to be a practicing Catholic, or even a Christian, to benefit from the power of prayer. Taking the time to quietly reflect on your life regardless of your belief system, or lack thereof, can have a huge impact. Building prayer into your day can relieve stress, help you maintain a positive attitude, improve your outlook on life, reduce ego, and promote humility.

Rewrite Your Story

You have every right to a life that's full, enriching, and joyous. Commit to eliminating negative thinking, unhealthy friendships, and unsatisfying circumstances from your life by rethinking what's possible. I'm certainly not suggesting that you can snap your fingers and expect that a new life has been magically created for you. Ultimately, you are the pilot in command of your own life. *You* are the only one who can take charge of the story. Accept that life isn't linear and even the best stories have several dark moments. When crafting your story, stay focused on the end goal, don't agonize over the missteps, and make sure your actions are in line with the ending you want for yourself. When contemplating the course of your life story, consider the following:

- What kind of legacy do you want to leave?

- What made you feel most fulfilled?

- What would you regret not doing?

- When do you feel most proud?

- Who has provided you with support?

- To what and whom are you grateful?

- Which habits do you need to remove and replace?

- Have you remained true to your values?

- What were your biggest lessons?

- What have you taught others?

- Do you have more to give?

Drag #3: Addictions of All Kinds

Addictions, including alcohol, painkillers, tobacco, and other drugs, will create an extraordinary amount of drag. Addictions have been known to damage communities and destroy families, and anyone suffering from serious addiction should seek the appropriate help immediately. Even "softer" addictions, like surfing the net, gambling, online shopping, gossiping, watching too much television, pornography, social media, eating chocolate, and drinking too much diet soda, may seem harmless but will impede your quest to CAVU. These sorts of addictions can cause health issues and present a risk to your relationships and bank account.

Oscar Award–winning actor Anthony Hopkins recently told a group of students at the University of California that he was "disgusted, busted, and not to be trusted" when he was drinking. As a young actor he was hungover so often that he was nearly impossible to work with. Hopkins went on to say, "Nothing ever satisfied me. It could be an ocean of booze. Nothing would satisfy me—work, success . . . never fills the cup." Hopkins was able to change his life when a woman from the twelve-step program Alcoholics Anonymous asked him, "Why don't you just trust in God?" At the time, Hopkins didn't believe in God (in a moment of synchronicity, it was his addiction that led him to a life of faith). His newly discovered faith allowed him to face the real demons in his life and finally to achieve sobriety; he's been sober for forty years. To free yourself from parasitic drag it is essential to acknowledge addictions. Ask yourself this question: Is there an addiction in your life that prevents you from being your best self? If there is, commit with God's help to make this change.

Drag #4: Ego

I am blessed to have a great friendship with golf legend Jack Nicklaus and his wife, Barbara. For the purposes of my investigation into this topic, Jack recently shared a powerful story with me about how parasitic drag impacted him early in his career.

Jack burst onto the PGA Tour in the early 1960s and enjoyed unprecedented success, winning seven major championships by the time he was thirty-one. Unfortunately, his ego started to get in the way. "I grew complacent and stopped putting in the effort required to win majors," he told me. Jack's lack of focus and preparation resulted in his not winning a major championship for three consecutive years. In a tragic turn of events, Jack's father died unexpectedly at the age of fifty-six. Jack was overcome with guilt, because he knew his dad's proudest moments were watching his son win majors; and with a stronger work ethic, Jack would have won more for his dad. But this tragedy would ultimately inspire him. He would forgive himself and shed the drag of guilt and ego and rededicate himself to the pursuit of his talent. Six months after his father's death, Jack would win the British Open in honor of his father, as well as ten more major championships. Thanks to the power of forgiveness, Jack broke through his own ego and went on to win more majors than any golfer in history.

Having a person to whom you aspire can help you stay focused on your goals. It doesn't matter if this person is a friend or family member or if you're inspired by someone famous whom you've never met. Allow yourself to be inspired by stories of people who have started with nothing, succeeded against all odds, overcome hardships, initiated a unique worldview, or bounced back from failure. Let their stories push you forward and serve as examples of what can be achieved through hard work and perseverance.

If you want the enlightenment that comes from CAVU, you need to accept that *you* are not what you do, where you work, what you look like, or how much money you have. You've been given your own unique gifts and can use them to build a life of impact, or you can waste them obsessing over the picture you want to present to the world. Would you rather be right, or do the right thing? To recalibrate your ego and put yourself in a place to experience CAVU, try the following to divert focus away from yourself:

- Practice listening. Make a point of asking other people about their lives, and don't just talk about yourself. Try asking three questions in a conversation before sharing an anecdote about your life.

- Congratulate others when they succeed, even if it stings your own achievements. Writing a letter or texting someone congratulations will make their day but will also get you in the habit of feeling like you are deserving of everything.

- Stop one-upping people. *This is never flattering.*

- Don't engage in any attention-seeking behaviors. Don't seek sympathy, fish for compliments, or be purposefully controversial.

- Resist the urge to compare yourself to someone else. Be open to accepting others' opinions and respecting their ideas.

- Always give credit where credit is due.

The Right Stuff

To achieve CAVU, you need to be aware of what you're filling yourself up with, and it needs to be *the right stuff.* In 1979, Tom Wolfe published the bestselling book of the same name, about the inner lives of astronauts (it would also become a hit movie directed by Philip Kaufman). "The right stuff" of book and film fame referred to qualities shared by the astronauts and test pilots back in the 1940s and 1950s, an "unspoken code of bravery and courage that compelled these men to ride on top of dangerous rockets."

I have tremendous respect for the pilots who risked their lives to make advancements in aviation, and flying today's F-16 can certainly be dangerous and requires bravery, but I believe the modern version of the right stuff goes beyond qualities of intellect, superior coordination, and machismo attitude. To have the right stuff today, you must have physical, emotional, and spiritual health.

I strive to be the best version of myself, which requires me to continually revise and re-aim my priorities to ensure that my actions reflect my real and best self. I have spent years replacing my drag with positive alternatives. It is impossible to create an all-inclusive list, but these are a few more of the truly transformational practices in my life:

- Exercise forty-five minutes a day, six days a week. The benefits are endless.

- Hydrate your body. Your entire body—cells, tissues, and organs—operates in the medium of water. Within minutes of your drinking a bottle of water, your blood and metabolic system pushes out fluid that is littered with metabolic waste. You should drink 50 percent of your body weight in fluid ounces. For example, if you weigh 150 pounds, you should aim for seventy-five ounces of water a day. Consider starting your day with water immediately upon waking; it's like a power wash for your insides. Tom Brady,

Super Bowl MVP, drinks thirty-plus glasses of
water per day!

■ Explore "flexitarianism." People think I made
this term up, but it's real. I live a dynamic lifestyle with a lot of travel. My goal is vegan, but
I don't hold myself to strict adherence. It's an
80 percent solution to a diet that consists of
plants—fruits, vegetables, grains, and legumes.
I avoid the processed foods and junk that are
so easily accessible today. Though I have not
transitioned to full-fledged vegan (I still enjoy
the occasional piece of fish), I have discovered
many benefits from altering my diet, such as
huge gains in energy and an overall feeling of
well-being. The psychology of nutrition is a new
field that has shed a powerful light on how eating impacts our happiness. The typical Western
diet contributes to depression and poor physical
health. If you are looking for immediate and lasting change in your life, look at the end of your
fork. Drs. Dean Ornish and Nobel Prize win-
ner Elizabeth Blackburn found that a vegan diet
caused more than five hundred genes to change
in only three months, turning on genes that
prevent disease and turning off those that cause

breast cancer, heart disease, prostate cancer, and other illnesses. Avoiding animal products also helps protect Mother Earth by reducing carbon emissions. For more on this, check out the book *How Not to Die* or the Netflix documentary *The Game Changers*.

- Take more walks. I love taking hikes with my family and service dog, Bravo. A long walk outside is invigorating, and the sounds and sights of nature create a natural balm for the soul. Studies show that spending time outside in green spaces can have tremendous health benefits, including a reduction in the stress hormone cortisol, a lower heart rate, lower blood pressure, lower cholesterol, and lower risk of diabetes. It's also possible that chemicals emitted by trees have a positive effect on our immune system and cell health.

- Engage in activities that stimulate your mind. Read books that challenge you or see movies that spark curiosity and motivation. Learn something new—a foreign language, coding, or a musical instrument. Incorporating a new hobby into your life can increase learning speeds and helps build myelin, the white matter in your brain that supports the learning process. Virtually all great leaders and successful individuals are avid readers on an unending quest for knowledge and personal improvement.

- Eliminate foul language. Swearing has become so common today that we are practically immune to curse words when we hear them on television, in movies and songs, or out in public. As the father of five daughters, I made the decision a few years ago to eliminate foul language in an attempt to set a positive standard for the character of the people they will seek out in their lives. I took the lead from one of America's greatest patriots and our first president. On August 3, 1776, General George Washington issued an order against profanity and deemed it conduct unbecoming:

> The General is sorry to be informed that the foolish, and wicked, practice of profane cursing and swearing (a Vice heretofore little known in an American Army) is growing into fashion; he hopes the officers will, by example, as well as influence, endeavour to check it, and that both they, and the men, will reflect, that we can have little hopes of the blessing of Heaven on

our Arms, if we insult it by our impiety, and folly; added to this, it is a vice so mean and low, without any temptation, that every man of sense, and character, detests and despises it.

- Prioritize sleep. There are many things that can rob you of a decent night's sleep—elevated cortisol from stress or unstable blood sugars, alcohol, caffeine, and blue light from electronic devices. Develop healthy sleep hygiene by avoiding caffeine too close to bedtime, incorporating movement and exercise into your lifestyle, making sure you're exposed to natural sunlight during the day, and ensuring that you have a relaxing and comfortable sleep environment. Chronic sleep loss can negatively impact your memory, ability to learn, metabolism and weight, mood, and cardiovascular health. Healthy sleep practices also boost your body's immune system.

6

Chair Flying

The United States of America spends billions of dollars training and preparing fighter pilots for battle, so it may surprise you to learn that one of our greatest training tools is a *plain old chair.*

At its core, "chair flying," as we call it, entails sitting down, closing one's eyes, and visualizing the entire sequence of flight in one's mind. I have been flying fighters for almost twenty years, and I still have the same $85 chair I bought on sale at Pottery Barn when I first began UPT. Before every sortie, I chair-fly from start to finish—visualizing the ground ops (starting the jet and pre-flight checks), radio calls, takeoff, weapons employment, communications, and the eventual landing. Additionally, I picture all of the potential emergencies (a fire, blown tire, engine or flight control problems) while reminding myself that preparing for these incidents could one day save my life. Just like actual flying, chair flying is a skill that requires practice, and its key is in making the stationary position feel as realistic as possible. I do my best to incorporate sight, sound, and smell; when I actuate the controls, I do it with precision and confidence. When I light the afterburners, raise the gear, lower the flaps, or step on the rudder, I feel the jet's reaction.

The concept of chair flying has a deeper purpose than just visualization, though. Fighter pilots build muscle memory, methodically going through each motion of a difficult task in a relaxed environment. When I was in UPT and was first introduced to chair flying by one of my instructors, I began with the most basic of ground operations. Instructors hardwired the placement of switches, the start sequence, and radio calls into my brain. Although this initial training seemed mundane, it was an indoctrination to the discipline that would provide the foundation for flawless execution in combat. The mindset I honed during chair flying would prove invaluable a few months after graduation when I was deployed to Iraq and was cleared to drop a bomb for the very first time.

There is zero room for error in this situation. Making a mistake when dropping a bomb, or *going kinetic,* can have devastating consequences for blue forces and civilians. But as stressful as my first combat drop was, I was prepared because I had dropped bombs from my chair more times than I could count. By the time I was 30,000 feet in the air, I had already reached what I like to call "learned effective," which occurs when one's preparation is so strong that one is in total control of a high-pressure situation. Learned effective is when a task is so ingrained that you can operate in a form of mental autopilot. There are few things more satisfying than facing a high-pressure situation with complete confidence because you have put in the work to be learned effective.

We all have high-pressure moments that we must face in work and in life, whether it's giving a big presentation or singing a solo in the church choir. When I was in eighth grade, I struggled with the pressure that came from playing competitive golf. My mom and my dad would urge me to "just relax," but their advice never helped. No matter how many times I'd try to relax by taking deeper breaths or lowering my shoulders, I'd continue to choke. I wrongly believed (as many of us do) that any failure I experienced on the golf course would reflect upon my value as a human being. I tied performance to my self-worth, and I suffered from what sports psychologists call *fear of failure.*

As I grew older and gained more experience by competing against people better than me, I learned to better manage my performance anxiety, but still I struggled under pressure. Fast forward years later to UPT where the pressure became more extreme than anything I had ever been through (including teeing it up against Tiger Woods in college). The USAF pilot training program was designed to take us to the breaking point so that we could start building the mental toughness required to fly fighters in combat. Our days were grueling. With report times at 0430, we would fly one or two sorties each day, followed by academic classes, including lessons on aerodynamics, weather, and pilot physiology. Every evolution was briefed, debriefed, and graded afterward, and we were under constant scrutiny by the instructors. Learning to fly the plane safely (while being lethal at the same time) required uncompromising discipline and dedication to learning, and the threat of being sent home due to poor performance loomed greatly. We were always a couple consecutive busted rides from washing out of the program.

In a moment of synchronicity, textbook academics would help me redefine my relationship with performance anxiety. One of our earliest lessons in ground academics covered Bernoulli's principle, which states that pressure beneath the wing combined with speed causes lower pressure on top of the wing, which ulti-mately makes the plane fly. In other words, *pressure equals lift.*

In terms of flight, pressure is an extraordinary gift. If pressure could lift a 32,000-pound F-16, imagine how it could mentally and physically lift ordinary peo-ple. Pressure was negatively bringing me down and, as a result, sabotaging my performance. I knew that if I wanted to make it through the most demanding and expensive training in the military, I'd have to learn how not to choke under pressure. If pressure was going to permeate my experience at UPT and beyond, I had to take control of it. If I didn't, it would forever define my fate. Could pressure be harnessed and used as a way to rise above the stress and help me reach my God-given potential?

LOE #5: Reach Learned Effective

Bernoulli's principle changed my perspective during my training. Instead of viewing pressure as the element that could make everything unravel, I'd start to accept it as the catalyst that can bring it all together. Instead of feeling unmoored and afraid, I would let pressure push me to become learned effective. The physical and mental sensations that stem from high-pressure situations would no longer spark anxiety but would trigger a much more realized set of thoughts, steeped in the present but aimed toward the future. You can start to change your relationship with pressure by running through these various thought processes when facing a high-stakes situation in work or life:

- I'm facing a high-pressure situation, but I will focus on the fact that there are rewards to be gained by making it through.

- I'm envisioning myself succeeding in this moment, and I know what that success looks like and feels like.

- I am prepared to handle this pressure because I've created a healthy routine that supports me both mentally and physically.

- The process of routine fuels the notion of learned effective.

- I know what can go wrong, but I have a plan for handling those scenarios.

- Pressure is a gift that God gives us to help us perform at the highest level.

All great accomplishments—running a marathon, winning a major championship in golf, dropping a bomb in combat, winning a court case, giving an important presentation at work, negotiating a raise, or performing onstage—stem from pressure. Pressure can cause stress—it almost always does—but when viewed as a necessary function it can also spark the desire to succeed and fuel the superhuman in all of us. To reach learned effective, wherein you perform exactly how you want to when faced with pressure, practice the following steps.

Step #1: Chair-Fly—Face the What-Ifs

Determined to make it through UPT, I spent hours chair flying in my home office. I'd settle into a quiet room, close my eyes, and run through every motion of a flight, including the good, the bad, and the what-ifs of a sortie. Allowing yourself to ponder your what-ifs, experience them in your mind, and decide upon your course of action in a safe space (it can't get much safer than a chair) will positively impact your performance. As you're sitting quietly in your chair, take a moment to calm your breathing, then let your mind run through each negative outcome. What course of action will you take if the worst happens?

What can you do right now from the safe space of your chair that won't be possible during the course of action?

Step #2: Positive Vision-Cast

Positive vision casting is also a function of chair flying, but this time you *only* visualize yourself succeeding. You've already gone through all of the what-ifs in your chair, and now it's time to let yourself go through the entire process, nailing the job every step of the way.

Many of the best athletes in the world vision-cast themselves winning before competing. Bob Bowman, who coached Michael Phelps, the most decorated Olympian of all time, incorporated visualization into Phelps's training. Phelps watched a "mental videotape" of his races before bed at night and first thing in the morning. He would visualize every part of the race, from the moment he stepped onto the starting block to diving into the water to, finally, his big win. Bowman believes that visualization helped create a pattern of success for Phelps. "We figured [imagery] was best to concentrate on these tiny moments of success and build them into mental triggers," he said. "It's more like his habits had taken over."

Similarly, the Olympic champion skier Lindsey Vonn visualizes the race more than a hundred times and incorporates physically shifting her weight with specific breathing patterns. Many of the best golfers in the world play every hole in their mind's eye before an important round. For me, visualization was something that I always used because it helped me relax. I'd feel the sun on my back as I got ready to tee up. I could feel my hands on the club and the turf under my feet, and I could see the ball flying through the air and landing exactly where I wanted it to. Whatever high-pressure task you're facing, run through its events. Visualize yourself succeeding, experience the feelings that success evokes, and let the joy of crushing it run through you.

Step #3: Create a Routine for Peak Performance

The military runs on routine. Routine creates order and requires discipline, both of which are essential for combat. A healthy routine is a crucial part of becoming learned effective because it builds self-confidence, boosts energy, sharpens focus, and helps you stay in control of your life. Over time, routine becomes automatic, but only if you stay the course.

0545	Prayer of gratitude to meet the day—this is the day the Lord has made!
0600	Workout time.
0715	Take all kids to school. Pray on way to school. This is a "nonnegotiable" in my schedule. I always take the kids to school and pick them up.
0800	Vegan shake.
0830	Attend daily mass, have coffee.
0915–1300	Work: meetings, emails, phone calls, writing, planning schedule, reviewing speeches.
1300	Devotional prayers, scripture. Send me your email and I will include you in my next round of prayers!
1300–1320	Quick healthy snack.
1320–1500	Work continues.
1530	Pick kids up from school.
1530–1700	Work and planning for the next day (this is important because it sets my expectations for the next day).
1700–2100	Family time: dinner, homework.
1730	Glass of red wine.
2100	Kids' bedtime routine: brush and floss teeth, tuck into bed, prayers.

| 2130 | Get in bed. Read the Bible for five minutes (just the act of opening the Bible brings me peace). Light candle, read or watch TV. |
| 2200 | Lights out. |

When creating your own routine, base it on your "nonnegotiables." Spend time thinking about what activities are essential to maintain a sense of well-being and *full*-fillment. As you incorporate these activities into your routine, it's important to include actions you enjoy or can easily accomplish, thereby creating a cycle of victories for yourself. These actions can increase in difficulty as you progress, but it's imperative that you do not begin with the impossible.

A healthy routine will have an enormously positive impact on your life. I will never forget the process of building my routine back when I was flying out of Sheppard Air Force Base in Texas, living with Jacqy and our two Dobermans, Bogey and Sosa. I had to build a routine that could keep up with the supersonic speeds I was flying over West Texas (not to mention that the street we lived on was called Speedway). Now that my life has grown to include five daughters, four jobs, and three dogs, I have altered it accordingly. While my daily routine changes slightly if I am traveling or flying fighters (I spend one week a month at Eglin Air Force Base in Florida flying in the 301st Fighter Squadron), when I'm at home my current peak-performance routine looks like this:

When I think back to when I was that nervous, perpetually stressed kid on the golf course, I never could have imagined that those same feelings of angst and uncertainty would someday fuel me to succeed. It took time, but with the help of Bernoulli and a learned effective routine, I overhauled my relationship with pressure. Flying the F-16 taught me that pressure is something to be appreciated and valued.

Do remember, though, that mastery does not mean avoidance. In late 2019, I was flying fighters down in New Orleans, and as I approached the jet for my last leg of the cross-country from New Orleans back to Tulsa, I felt it again . . . that well-known sensation of nerves. The pressure that comes from flying a supersonic fighter jet is *still* something I feel before every sortie, but now I view it as signal. The pressure reminds me that I've done the work, I'm learned effective and ready to face a mission's myriad challenges. The day that I don't react from pressure is the day that I hang my flight suit up permanently, and that day will be one of the scariest of them all.

7

EM Curve

The demands of modern life can be overwhelming. From careers to commutes to child care to extracurriculars, our daily tasks have a habit of taking up most of our time and draining us of our energy. But if you're going to bed at night exhausted and notice that your first thought upon waking is, *How will I get everything done?* your problem isn't your to-do list; it's how you're managing your energy.

Like many people, I am susceptible to measuring my energy level in proportion to the tasks I need to accomplish. My typical day could include anything from attending an important event for Folds to flying fighter jets to shuttling the kids home from soccer games and dance recitals. As the pace of my life has increased over the years, I discovered that the energy-maneuverability

(EM) theory—the same principle I used to manage the energy of my jet during flight—could provide a solution to the modern issue of busy schedules.

The concept of the EM theory originates with John Boyd, who flew an F-86 during the Korean War, then graduated top of his class at the prestigious Fighter Weapons School, where he became an instructor. In addition to his spearheading the revolutionary design of the F-15 and F-16, he is known as one of the greatest military theorists in U.S. history.

In the early 1960s, Boyd collaborated with civilian mathematician Thomas Christie to create the energy-maneuverability theory of aerial combat. In the fighter-pilot world, this theory translates to *how to manage energy in order to kill and survive in a dogfight*. A successful kill can be traced back nearly 100 percent of the time to the pilot who enters the fight at corner velocity at a speed of 430–450 knots (F-16 corner) and properly manages their energy in relation to the other aircraft. The pilot who flies in the smallest circle at the quickest pace will win the dogfight. The fastest rate combined with the smallest circle equals *peak efficiency*, and in a dogfight, peak efficiency allows the pilot to enter the control zone perfectly positioned behind the other pilot's jet. The best regime to employ the gun or air-to-air missile. *Win!*

Flying combat over Iraq, prepared to deliver the president's mail.

Colonel Randy "Tractor" Cason giving me the oath
for my promotion to lieutenant colonel.

Flying T-38 Talons out of Eglin.
Best mulligan of my life.

My girls understand that freedom is not free. So proud to walk with them at Folds of Honor.

The American Dunes team *(left to right):* Jacqy, me, Mom, Barbara Nicklaus, Dad, and Jack Nicklaus.

All my girls.

Lifting the Folds of Honor QuikTrip 500 trophy with our Folds recipients *(left to right)* Ryann, Wesley, and Ellie—the family of Major Larry Bauguess, KIA 2007.

Jacqy is my wingman for life.

The Great American Lager. Budweiser has donated more than $18 million to Folds of Honor.

Danica is a true inspiration and hero of faith.

Two awesome guys who have been with me since the beginning: Rickie Fowler and David Feherty.

Getting ready to fly a mission with Otter over Iraq in 2008.

Me and Bravo, my service dog provided by our partners at K9s for Warriors.

Colonel Brian "Jethro" Neil flew the longest combat mission in history. The most inspiring leader I ever worked for in the USAF.

The power of volition with Gary Woodland and Amy Bockerstette.

Met my best brother, Gavin Hadden, on my first *Fox & Friends* story with President Bush. We have been changing lives together ever since.

Proud to award a Folds scholarship to Medal of Honor recipient Leroy Petry's family. Larry the Cable Guy is a true supporter of our mission.

Flying a sortie with the 301st Fighter Squadron over the Gulf of Mexico.

Honored to serve with President Bush 43.

At the Patriot Cup proudly wearing Volition America. "God and Country with No Apologies."

I studied and applied Boyd's theory extensively in the air, but I also learned to understand how I could use it to manage my life on the ground. Boyd's theory emphasizes efficiency to avoid ending up on what fighter pilots call the back side of the EM curve. This happens when a pilot fails to properly meld thrust, vertical energy (fighting downhill), and G-forces. The jet can quickly slow down and feel "mushy" in the air and unresponsive to the pilot's input. On the back side of the EM curve, inefficiency leads to the lack of performance, and suddenly a jet is in the weakest possible position to win the fight.

LOE #6: EM CURVE

Like jets, if humans don't utilize their available energy carefully, they can end up on the back side of the EM curve. If you're not being mindful of how you manage your energy, you can fall behind and feel as if it's impossible to catch up.

I realize that it is impossible to remain on a perfect EM curve all the time. There are unexpected disruptions that require energy and immediate attention, whether it's putting out a fire at work, personal issues, or needing to pick up a sick child from school. Unexpected circumstances and sudden change require us to double- or even triple-task, which of course drains our mental capacity and wears us down. In these moments, we dig deep, but most of the time we operate under a "normal" battle rhythm of life, so let's keep our discussions focused on normal ops.

When I'm energy-deficient in the jet, I *unload.* To unload the jet, I roll out and push the stick forward. This takes the energy-draining weight of the G-force off the jet, allowing it to pick up airspeed and get back on the proper side of the EM curve. It's important that we take time to unload in life too. These days, I spend about half of my time on the road working with partners of Folds of Honor, doing speaking engagements, and flying jets down in Florida. Sometimes I travel to four or five cities in a single week, only to get home for a night or two and head back out on the road toward my next venture. I'm blessed to have abundant work that I love, but it can be draining. No matter which hat I'm wearing while I'm working, the emails, phone calls, texts, and obligations bombard me at such a rate that it's difficult to balance my professional and personal lives. I used to come home from the airport completely wiped out and then head straight to my office. Jumping right into action only drained me even more, and before I knew it I was missing workouts, drinking too much coffee, and falling out the back side of the EM curve. It was having a negative impact on my family life. If I wanted to attain CAVU, I needed to approach my reentry differently. Now, instead of killing myself to catch up, I unload. I manage my calendar, put away my cell phone, let myself grab a nap to feel recharged, play nine holes, get in a workout, or go for a walk with my family.

You too should take time to think through what you can unload in your life. We call it "slow down to speed up." You may think your practice of staying up until 2300 answering emails keeps you ahead of the game, but if your brain is reeling from the stimulation and you're not getting to sleep at a reasonable hour, the subsequent burnout you'll incur will be even more severe. When you find yourself with that mushy feeling on the back side of the EM curve, you have to take a break. Assess what's really important and have the faith in God to let the other stuff go. Say no and reschedule your meeting or cancel a social obligation; everything will be waiting for you when you reenter, I promise. Our work will be there until *death do us part* from it.

In a dogfight I am constantly adjusting my airspeed in the HUD, looking for energy-saving moments. As I worked to keep CAVU in my life I realized that I needed to do the same on the ground. Where in my life could I grab an extra pocket of energy?

I brought the same discipline and cross-check to my life that I used in the cockpit. I thought through every social event and obligation the same way, making sure my precious energy gets a proportional return on the investment. If it's not worth my energy, I unload it. We can't be everywhere and do everything, as much as we'd like to—it's a quick and easy recipe for eventual collapse. Learn to manage your energy by harnessing it, making it work *for you*.

Align Your Life with the Jet Stream

There are certainly times when you need to unload, but overall, I firmly believe that a life that is abundant with family, work, and social obligations is a blessing. Having places to go, people to see, and things to do are all signs that you are prospering! I am grateful every day for my family, my career flying fighters, my speaking engagements, and my work with Folds of Honor. Can it be exhausting sometimes? Sure! I've just shared that I have to unload at times, but that doesn't mean I'm going to give up on meaningful pursuits.

While there are clear theories about how to manage the energy of a jet, there's not a perfect formula for managing the challenges of daily life. We must accept and embrace that life is busy. Stop using your mental energy to try to slow down; that's like flying against the jet stream—you'll face nothing but resistance. In-stead, learn to let the jet stream push you along; you'll stay on the right side of the EM curve and will be able to enjoy all of blessings God has bestowed upon you. To align yourself with the jet stream, consider the fol-lowing.

Rank and Order

The military indoctrinated me into the world of rank and order. Translate the meaning of this into regular life and it refers to the art of prioritizing.

An in-flight emergency is never a good thing. Should there ever be a fire or a wounded bird,* it would be easy for an undisciplined pilot to devote their brainpower to dealing with the problem, ultimately causing them to forget that they need to actually *fly the plane.* That's why lesson number one in UPT is *aviate, navigate,* and *communicate.* Every USAF aviator has these hallowed words burned into their souls. In other words, fly the jet, navigate the jet, and then communicate your inten-tions as necessary. Failure to follow this flow has killed thousands of aviators.

As I've developed CAVU, I've learned what I require to fully function as a person (in my case it's prayer, ex-

---

* An aircraft damaged by enemy fire.

ercise, healthy foods, work, flying, family time, fellowship with the bros, getting outside, and spending time with my dog, Bravo). And if my ops tempo is so out of control that I can't "aviate," I need to take a hard look at everything on my radar. I need to consider which tasks are crucial and which ones can be pushed off until later. I need to determine what I can get rid of so I can "navigate" myself properly. Once I've determined what I can do, what I can't, and what needs to happen later, I'll communicate that information to the necessary people involved.

Recharge

I grew up attending Catholic mass every Sunday with my parents. While we didn't observe the sabbath in its strictest capacity, Sundays felt different from the rest of the week. We'd get up early, eat breakfast together, put on our good church clothes, and pile into the car for mass. Growing up, our Sundays were more about *togethering*. After mass, we'd spend time with other parishioners, having conversations over coffee and a weird, dry breakfast cake that disintegrated in your hands. The dry breakfast cake didn't matter because it was fellowship that warmed our souls. Sundays weren't about frantically running errands (many stores were actually closed) and catching up on emails and watching YouTube; they were about communion and commonality.

Fast forward to today, with a life replete with work obligations and five daughters who do countless activities, and Sunday is just as fast-paced as every other day. Sure, we attend mass together as a family, but Sunday has lost that feeling of peace, quietude, and togetherness. One of my favorite bands, Rascal Flatts, who I am blessed to call good friends and brothers in Christ, perform a song called "Mayberry" that beautifully captures the lost spirit of the Sabbath in one line of its lyrics: *Sunday was a day of rest, now it's one more day for progress.* I had actually begun to find myself feeling melancholy on Sundays, and I know that it's because I was in conflict with the Bible's command. Just like everyone else, I was trying to pack it all in rather than respecting a full-on day of rest.

> *There are six days when you may work, but*
> *the seventh day is a day of sabbath rest, a day*
> *of sacred assembly. You are not to do any work;*
> *wherever you live, it is a sabbath to the Lord.*
> *(Leviticus 23:3)*

On a quest to recharge, my family and I had a simple revelation. Let's reconnect to the sabbath. We have gotten much more intentional about fighting for the sabbath. As a busy dad who spends a big part of Sunday afternoons shuttling girls from soccer games to dance recitals, I can't reasonably spend the day at home in quiet contemplation, but I can use it to consciously recharge. After the games are over and we're all home together, we'll turn off all our devices and have an early dinner. We'll enjoy a family kickball game, or maybe play nine holes or a game of Uncle Wiggily. My girls sometimes complain that this is "mandatory" fun, but it's so important to put on the speed brake on Sunday. Taking this small step in life can create positive energy and recharge us in biblical proportions.

There's no doubt about it: Achieving CAVU requires energy management. But you won't experience the joys and benefits of CAVU if you are constantly dragging behind and on the verge of running out of fuel. A life full of friends, family, work and social obligations is not something that should be slowed down but something that *can be managed* for peak efficiency and enjoyment. Manage your EM curve and push beyond your perceived limitations and you will discover a new level of energy you never knew existed.

8

Service Before Self

It was June 2006, and I was making the last leg of my trip, from Chicago to Grand Haven, Michigan, where I was going to work as a PGA Professional at the Grand Haven Golf Club. Grand Haven is a beautiful town on the eastern shore of Lake Michigan where families gather during the summer to enjoy the sandy white beaches, take strolls along the boardwalk to the famous red lighthouse, fish, hike, and enjoy ice-cream cones en route through the picture-perfect downtown after dinner. My love for Grand Haven stretches back all the way to 1998, the year my dad and I managed to pull together a group of investors and purchase the Grand Haven Golf Club, now known as American Dunes.

As I boarded the plane, I took a quick peek inside the cockpit, a sight I never grow weary of. On the way to my seat, I walked by a young soldier wearing dress greens who was sitting quietly in first class. I remember thinking that he was probably going home on leave and was pleased someone had taken care of him by getting him an upgrade. But once I settled into my seat in coach and looked out the window at the bright lights of the airport, I forgot about the soldier altogether.

I have always loved airports at night. There is something magical about watching planes taking off into the vast blanket of dark sky. There is also the mystery that magic contains: Where are all those planes going? And what kinds of lives do their passengers have?

Inside the Boeing 737, the engines roared to life as we prepared to take off. On our climb-out, I admired the John Hancock Building peeking out through the clouds, its maze of crossbeams pointing toward infinity. The skies were angry that night. The turbulence made me reminisce about the training flights I used to take across the desolate plains of Texas in the T-38 Talon, a two-seat supersonic trainer the Air Force uses to shape the next generation of fighter pilots. In the T-38 instrument phase we learned how to fly in clouds and at night with our instruments as our only guide, a grueling test of how to *think* while traveling 500 miles per hour. This skill can be trained and tested, but ultimately it's built into pilots' DNA or it's not. The instrument phase is where most wannabe fighter pilots wash out.

The chime of the seat belt sign interrupted my wandering thoughts. United 664 was beginning its descent into Grand Rapids, just twenty minutes after we had taken off. As we taxied to the gate, the captain made an announcement. "We have an American hero on board with us tonight."

I thought back to the soldier sitting in first class. I wondered what brave act he had accomplished.

After a long pause the captain continued, "We are carrying the remains of Army corporal Brock Bucklin. His twin brother, Corporal Brad Bucklin, is in first class and has brought him home."

Only a few months earlier I had returned from my second tour of duty in Iraq and thought that I had left the death and destruction of the war behind. But hearing this tragic news made me feel like the war had followed me home. I thought of the sacrifice Brock Bucklin had made for this country, as well as the sadness his brother must've been holding. The captain made another request: "I'd like everyone on board to please remain seated as a sign of respect until Brock

Bucklin's remains are removed from the aircraft," he said. This was the least we could do as Americans to honor this young man and his family.

For the next thirty minutes I watched with reverence as a hero's ceremony unfolded outside the aircraft. The Bucklin family stood on the tarmac, holding on to each other, while flashes of light from emergency vehicles illuminated the darkness. Brock Bucklin's casket descended the cargo hold ramp, covered lovingly in the American flag—the swaths of red, white, and blue representing the true meaning of his sacrifice. Nearby was Brock's small son, his eyes fixed on his father's casket. As a father myself, I couldn't imagine what was going through his young mind.

The honor guards raised their white, luminous gloves over Brock's remains. Meanwhile, Brock's twin brother had left his seat in first class and joined the honor guards to help carry his brother, who had come home for the very last time.

I had seen the horrors of war firsthand from the cockpit of my F-16 and the hospital in Balad, but I had never seen this side of the war. I watched the Bucklins on the darkest night of their lives. As the family held on to each other, I couldn't help but wonder how my own family would react if it were me who came home in a casket. I thought of the relationship I share with my dad and what an important role model and source of wisdom he has always been. I thought of my sleeping daughters, whom I'd kiss on the forehead when I returned home. And finally, I thought of the child on the tarmac who'd have to go through life without his father. I knew that there were thousands of other children just like him who had lost a parent in service to their country, but this fact is hard to contextualize unless you're observing this grief in real time.

I had been so absorbed in the homecoming of Corporal Brock Bucklin that I didn't notice what else was taking place around me. When I finally turned from the window back to the cabin, I was sickened by what I saw. Many of the passengers aboard United 664 had ignored the captain's request to stay seated and had left. I knew we were the last flight to arrive at the airport in Grand Rapids; there were no connecting flights to catch or anywhere else for anyone to go other than the comfort of their own homes. They could sleep safely under a warm blanket of freedom thanks to the sacrifices made by soldiers like Brock Bucklin. I felt anger welling inside me, while at the same time refusing to believe that so many people had callously and deliberately turned their backs on Brock and his family. I wanted to believe that most Americans understood that freedom was not free.

At that moment a powerful force—call it common duty, call it something bigger—stirred me to action. I felt God's hand on my shoulder; HE picks the least among us, but I was ready to serve. I didn't know exactly what I was going to do or even where to start, but I knew that I had to help that family. What could I do to ease their burden? How could I help ensure that this brave soldier's sacrifice wouldn't be forgotten?

God was calling me on a mission. I walked off the plane, up the jet bridge, and called my wife, Jacqy, to tell her about my experience and game-changing moment of synchronicity. When I explained what I had seen that night, Jacqy wholeheartedly agreed to support me on my newfound calling.

LOE #7: Service Before Self

For you have been called to live in freedom,
my brothers and sisters. But don't use your
freedom to satisfy your sinful nature. Instead,
use your freedom to serve one another in love.
(Galatians 5:13)

There are three core values that we adhere to in the Air Force:

- Integrity first

- Excellence in all we do

- Service before self

While the first two values are about character, service before self refers to the dedication each individual airman displays by putting his country before his own life, putting aside individual needs and comforts for the sake of others, and making complete and necessary sacrifices in defense of the U.S. Constitution. While I was very much accustomed to the concept of service before self from my many years in the Air Force (only half a percent of the population suits up each day for the U.S. military to protect the other 99.5 percent), that moment on Flight 664 extended the idea of service beyond my chosen vocation. While I was proud of my service to my country, I aspired to deepen my commitment to serving others.

As it turned out, Jesus would be my ultimate inspiration as I began to think about how I could help Brock Bucklin's family. Jesus may have been the son of God, but he was sent to earth to serve, not to be served. He worked effortlessly with the sick and poor (who were often shunned by others) by healing their wounds and providing them with food and the comfort of kind words.

After witnessing that scene on the tarmac, I wanted to open my heart, mind, and spirit to the Bucklin family. I wanted to find a way to ease their burden. And if I could help the Bucklins, perhaps I could also help other families who were facing similar struggles and make a difference that would have a truly lasting impact.

Inspiration Without Action Is Meaningless

It is one thing to feel inspired—who hasn't seen a terrible news story about a deadly disaster and felt compelled to help?—but it's quite another thing to channel inspiration into action. I was inspired to help Brock's young son, but I wanted to pursue an action that resulted in lifelong change. Sure, I could have written a check or started a fund for Brock's son (who I would soon learn was named Jacob and was only four years old when his father died), but what about the next family? After much contemplation, discussion, and prayer, Jacqy and I started Folds of Honor above our garage in Broken Arrow, Oklahoma. Our mission was simple and has never wavered: to honor the sacrifice of our fallen and disabled service members by providing educational scholarships to their children and spouses. We wanted to ensure that Jacob, and others like him, had the opportunity to get an education (we provide scholarships from first grade through college) and pursue the American dream that his father had given his life to protect. These scholarships would also serve as a reminder to civilians that we have a duty to honor the sacrifices made by those who preserve the freedom we so easily take for granted.

During a formative and challenging time at Folds, I received a letter that pushed me forward. It was from Matthew and Daniel Cash, and it described how their favorite memory was playing golf with their dad, before he was killed in Iraq. To remember him, they would pull out old scorecards and recount the time with him on the golf course. This letter touched me. For one thing, it was yet another example of how golf would continue to manifest itself in synchronistic ways. But more importantly, it showed me the power of also using Folds to help foster positive memories; without money to worry about, spouses and children could spend more time living in their honored traditions. I am proud to say that Matthew and Daniel are both Folds of Honor graduates and that they continue to pay tribute to their father, Army captain Chris Cash, who gave his life for our freedoms. It took years of hard work by many dedicated patriots, but Folds grew from a tiny organization to the largest military scholarship foundation in America. Since that moment of synchronicity, as of 2019 we have awarded over twenty-five thousand scholarships worth $125 million to the dependents of U.S. military members who have been killed or permanently disabled.

Putting service before self does not require that you rent an office, hire a staff, and start your own nonprofit. It doesn't even require you thinking in grandiose terms. But incorporating an element of service into your life can be life altering. My work with Folds has brought wonderful people into my world, newfound amazing friendships with our donors, former presidents, celebrities, and extraordinary young Americans who use Folds scholarships to do great things. While Folds has risen to unexpected heights, I believe that being driven by service on *any level* brings tremendous benefits.

The Jewish faith calls acts of kindness *tikkun olam*, which translates as "world repair." Jewish people believe that human beings have a responsibility to right what is wrong in the world, and that any *tikkun* performed helps spread positivity to the rest of the world. Every random act of kindness, no matter the size, multiplies into more good and brings the world closer to a harmonious state. To begin your journey of service of any size, consider the following.

Let Your Passions Guide You

I knew immediately that I wanted to contribute to the education of the families of our fallen soldiers, but there was one big problem. How exactly was I going to raise donations?

I had an idea: I would use golf, the game I loved most, to help me. I made a call to the PGA of America and explained my idea for a fund-raiser called Patriot Golf Day, the concept being that an event would take place at golf courses nationwide on Labor Day (now Memorial Day). The president of the PGA of America, Brian Whitcomb, got right on board, and our first fund-raiser brought in $1.1 million. Fast forward twelve years, and Patriot Golf Day is now the biggest grassroots sports fund-raiser in golf's history.

While golf provided a big solution to an immediate problem, incorporating golf into my service work also made it much more meaningful. Playing golf is one of my greatest passions, but marrying the game with the good work of raising $50 million for college educations is beyond anything I could have imagined. Golf has manifested itself in ways that I can't fully articulate; almost every significant moment in my life is connected directly to the game. I met a fighter pilot for the first time on the golf course when I was twelve, which inspired me to join the Air Force. My local PGA Pro encouraged me to pursue my dream of becoming a Class A PGA Professional. I went to the University of Kansas to play golf, where I met my wife. I was on my way to my job as a PGA Professional on the flight with the Bucklins. Yet again, I would turn to the game I love as a catalyst to start Folds of Honor. Bob Philion at Puma Golf would embrace the idea for Volition America, and we would win on golf's biggest stage, the U.S. Open.

I never thought of Folds as a "project" or as something to cross off my to-do list. I felt deeply passionate about helping the families of our fallen soldiers: I am constantly coming up with new ideas to try, people to get involved with, and ways to expand. Folds is my life's calling.

Service is a way of life, but you're more likely to make an impact if your work mirrors your own passions. Start by asking yourself questions about your passions, hobbies, and interests, and then use the answers to elevate your excitement and better define your goals. What issues are close to your heart? Where do you think you can make a direct impact? And finally, will this work sustain you?

Just Because You're "Doing Good" Doesn't Mean It'll Be Easy

Make no mistake, we faced many trials as we built Folds. I could write a book on all the challenges of establishing a nonprofit—board of directors, compliance, HR, awarding scholarships, marketing, donor services, missteps along the way—but the specifics aren't what matters. The real question is: Do you have the conviction in your heart to stay the course? It is the rarest of gifts to be able to combine what you do with who you are. I am living proof that conviction can keep you on track.

It's important to be up-front with yourself about expectations. Every day, I am aware that there are students currently enrolled in college who are expecting those tuition bills to be paid by Folds every semester. While I deeply wish we could help every single person, I know that is not feasible. Push yourself, but be aware of your limits. Understand that as deep as your passion may run, and as hard as you might work, you won't be able to change everyone's lives. Instead of focusing on what I can't change, I think about the positive change that Folds *has* created. I think about the students who are approaching graduation, or who are about to start a new chapter of their lives, and feel grateful that our organization was able to play a role.

The Minute You Start Helping Others, You're Actually Helping Yourself

Bringing a practice of service into life generates real change and provides a gateway to living a fulfilled life. There is also a significant amount of evidence that serving others ultimately serves you. Ever felt a sort of "rush" after performing a good deed? That sensation is known as "helper's high" and is produced when your brain releases endorphins, the feel-good chemicals of the brain. Doing good increases health and life expectancy, promotes mental wellness, fosters happiness, and even motivates you to continue the good deeds. A 2013 Carnegie Mellon study found that two hundred hours of volunteering per year correlated to lower blood pressure among the volunteers. In another study, researchers from the University of Buffalo found a link between giving, unselfishness, and a lower risk of early death. Furthermore, after an extensive review of forty studies on the effect of volunteering, BioMed Central concluded that volunteering is good for mental health, improves well-being and life satisfaction, and is linked to a decrease in depression.

Watching Brock Bucklin's ceremony on the runway was one of the saddest moments of my life, but it also provided me with one of my greatest gifts. Brock's son, Jacob, is only now old enough to start college, and knowing that he can pursue his dreams without the burden of paying for school is something that gives me strength and fills me with daily purpose. Though CAVU is a lifelong pursuit, full of many obstacles and nonstop work, the evolution of *service before self* will change you in unimaginable ways. As long as you're open to the possibilities that a life of service can bring to you, you are open to having your life permanently altered for the good.

9

Sons of Thunder

The U.S. Air Force has special-use airspace in the Gulf of Mexico, where pilots execute war exercises and test a variety of weapon systems. These spaces are called military operating areas (MOAs) and comprise hundreds of square miles off the coast of the Florida Panhandle. In the MOA, we are permitted to operate from the surface up to 60,000 feet with no airspeed limitations. We can fly supersonic, shoot missiles, and deploy countermeasures such as chaff* or flares.†

---

* A small cloud of glass fiber or plastic that hides aircraft from radar-guided missiles.
† Flares are composed of magnesium, with a burning temperature hotter than jet exhaust, to decoy against enemy IR missiles.

These vast MOAs serve as the home of the Weapon System Evaluation Program (WSEP). The exercises allow WSEP to ensure that the pilots and weapons perform under the pressure of actual live-fire conditions. During standard training sorties, we simulate firing missiles. With the help of sophisticated debriefing tools, we can assess whether the missile would have hit the other aircraft, although there is no way to 100 percent validate the shot. But at WSEP, I had the once-in-a-career opportunity to shoot a live AIM-120 AMRAAM.* In this high-pressure arena, I got to test myself and the Air Force weapon system, and managers had a forum to verify the system performance, capabilities, and limitations of the missile.

It was February, and the winter weather patterns presented some serious challenges for our sorties.

We brief air-to-air training rules before each sortie that are designed to keep our missions as safe as possible. One of the most critical training rules we follow is to *always have a discernible horizon*. In the dynamic regime of high speed, high G, and inverted flight attitudes, a discernible horizon helps us immediately decipher up versus down. Trust me, it can be hard to

---

* An American beyond-visual-range radar-guided air-to-air missile capable of all-weather operations day or night.

comprehend which way is up or down, and it's especially difficult during the winter, when rain and fog affect visibility and we commonly experience the "milk bowl" effect. This happens when hazy conditions cause the ocean and sky to become a mirror image of each other. We have to be extremely vigilant while flying in the milk bowl because it can be nearly impossible to determine the orientation of the jet. The bubble canopy of the F-16 has blessed me with the most majestic views of my life, but it is also the perfect environment for *spatial-D*. The Viper is such a perfect flying machine, and in the weather it can feel motionless. Without a proper cross-check of your instruments, you can become spatially disoriented and find yourself in a dangerous or deadly situation.

It was a milk bowl morning as we took off out of Tyndall Air Force Base. I was nervous as we pressed into the airspace with a live AIM-120 on my wing— cost: $1.1 million.

Tribe 1, turn left 180 climb to 11,000—cleared into whiskey 151.

Just a couple minutes after takeoff, we were established in the confines of the MOA. We checked in with range control and I quickly ran another BIT (built-in test) check on the missile to make sure it was ready to shoot.

Tribe 1 target bullseye 180-65 . . .

I moved the cursor on my air-to-air radar to that location and waited impatiently for the QF-4* remote-controlled drone to appear on my radar screen. I pushed forward on the stick with my right thumb so my APG-65 radar would put more energy in that location. The QF-4 appeared as a small gray square and I locked on.

Tribe 1 targeted 180-30 . . .

I pressed down on the red pickle button and looked out to my right wing. Flames shot from the missile's motor as it quickly separated from my F-16. I was traveling at Mach 1.1, but the powerful AIM-120 made me feel like I was standing still. I watched its arcing climb into the pale gray sky, and as the missile went out of sight I snipped (broke) my lock on the QF-4.

The AMRAAM is unique because pilots don't have to support it with a radar lock until it hits the target; it is a fire-and-forget missile. But I will never forget that day. As I continued to fly south, I began to see . . . a fireball spinning sideways? *What in the world?* I thought. It quickly became clear that my AMRAAM had malfunctioned and I was now traveling much faster than it! Within seconds, I caught up

---

* A reusable, remotely piloted aerial target that provides a realistic full-scale target for air-to-air weapon systems evaluation.

SONS OF THUNDER · 135

to the out-of-control missile and it helicoptered just a few feet over my canopy. I was almost the first pilot in history to shoot himself down.

Tribe 1—knock it off!

On the flight back to base, I replayed the bizarre and somewhat terrifying events in my mind. My mistake had nothing to do with the missile going stupid, but with my violating a training rule. I had locked the correct target, but in my excitement fired before I received clearance from the range control. It all turned out fine, but my young fighter-pilot ego was bruised after a very long debrief.

One of the primary reasons why the fighter-pilot community is so effective is that we walk into the debrief and check our egos at the door. The debrief is a time-honored tradition that calls for brutal and honest feedback. One of the most valuable lessons I have learned in our community is taking responsibility for our mistakes and not making excuses. We call this *owning it*.

The skies over the Gulf of Mexico may have been a milk bowl the day of my missile shoot at Tyndall, but there is a bright and clear light of integrity that permeates our business. Outside of that environment, the rest of the world's moral horizon is frequently clouded, and the difference between right and wrong is often poorly adjusted to fit our personal situations. Look no further than your local news channel to see how our perspective about the world is shaped by negative stories; even sadder is the fact that we thrive on hearing these examples, using them as counterweights to our own experiences. The notion of watching people fail is a sad footnote of our society. We should be celebrating when others succeed, rooting them on, yet we are so quick to go against our humanitarian instincts.

During one of my biggest trials, I struggled to keep sight of my moral horizon. It was the first big wreck of my life and it took place at The Patriot, the ambitious golf course project I started in Owasso, Oklahoma, designed by famous golf course architect Robert Trent Jones Jr. on an exquisite but challenging piece of land. It started with zero dollars and a dream, but with the help of my dad I had managed to put together forty-five founding members and finances to build it. One year into our construction, and while I was halfway around the world in Iraq, the Great Recession had hit. When I returned to Tulsa, I should have been out of the fight. Instead, I found myself in a new battle to save a golf course that was months behind schedule and 50 percent over budget, with my remaining funds set to run out in sixty days.

In my desperation, I entered the milk bowl. My pride got the best of me and my first instinct was to spin the situation in defense of myself, my family, and my finances. It took time to find my moral horizon, but I ultimately found the courage to fail. I owned it. The Patriot was going down and I was going down with it. *I needed help.* Humility and the truth, as they so often do, inspired unity. Thankfully, my partners, Paul, Sanjay, David, Tom, and Dad, stayed the course and stayed together. I am proud that today The Patriot is thriving.

> Courage is not simply one of the virtues but the form of every virtue at the testing point, which means at the point of highest reality. Without courage, men and women will fail to be loving, to sacrifice, to count the cost, to tackle the challenges or take on the responsibilities that God calls them to. **—C. S. Lewis**

It's easy to do the right thing when you are flying in CAVU skies, but flying in the milk bowl requires courage and deep character. Yet all around us are abundant examples of companies and individuals who choose to preserve their ego and image over their integrity.

Look at giant companies like Enron, Volkswagen, Bear Stearns, and Boeing. The actions they took when things went wrong made their situations worse, and in some cases unrecoverable.

One of my heroes, Lance Armstrong, inspired me with his many accomplishments on a bike and through the good works of his foundation. But when it was uncovered that he had been using performance-enhancing drugs, instead of taking responsibility, he tried to justify his actions by explaining that this was a widespread phenomenon in his sport. He had lost his moral horizon. The fallout that resulted is one from which he will likely never fully recover.

Be accountable and humble, and do your best to make it right. Own it just like we do in the fighter-pilot debrief.

LOE #8: *Faith Forward*

You will encounter situations that vector you into the milk bowl. Be aware of losing sight of the moral horizon and fight against the urge to justify or compromise your actions. When I was struggling to find a way out of my own personal milk bowl, it was clear that my faith was not strong enough. While reading scripture one night, I encountered the story of James and John in

Mark 3:16–17—yet another example of synchronicity, as this passage came to me at a time when I subconsciously screamed out for help.

I would discover that James and John were unique among the twelve apostles in their tendency to say whatever was on their minds. It was this kind of gusto that prompted Jesus to give them the name Boanerges, which means "sons of thunder." Jesus did this so that they might become thunderous and courageous men *of faith* instead of pursuing their own selfish ideas, as they had previously done.

Over the course of their lives, James and John became transformed by their love of God and learned to share their faith with the world. John would go on to write of Jesus's origins, his preachings, his acts of performing miracles, and his trial, crucifixion, and resurrection in the Gospel of John. The "apostle of love," as he is called, uses Jesus's lessons to demonstrate love and equity. James also went on to live a life of service to Jesus. He remained outspoken, but this time by spreading Jesus's message.

I was inspired by these brothers' transformation and dedication to something bigger than themselves. They pushed aside their own desires and fully committed themselves to spreading the word of Jesus Christ. They achieved virtuous acts as a result of their connection to their lifelong horizon. I too thought of myself as a "faithful" Christian who attended Catholic mass weekly with my family, but I realized I rarely shared my faith outside the confines of my local parish. Was I just going through the motions? Was my sense of faith deep enough to keep me from ending up in the milk bowl again? I wanted to dig deep and become a "thunderous and courageous man of faith," and made the choice to craft a "faith-forward" life.

We live in a society where sharing our religious beliefs has become politically incorrect. It takes courage to live a faith-forward life, but, inspired by the modern-day sons of thunder, I decided that the most effective way of stepping out in faith was to combine the good word with the doing of good deeds: Martin Luther King was a Christian minister who had a dream of racial equality, and he rallied a nation to end segregation, poverty, and the Vietnam War; Ross Perot joined in the Vietnam fight with his tireless efforts to bring home POWs; I loved how Pope Francis demonstrated faith-forwardness by breaking away from the traditions of living lavishly, which showed a high level of empathy with the poor. For most of us, dedicating one's life entirely to a single cause is not practical, but one can make a commitment to incorporate faith through words and works into everyday life. Our founding fathers are another great example of individuals who had "day jobs" but who committed themselves to service. The founding fathers led faith-forward lives (nearly half who signed the Declaration of Independence had seminary educations) and referenced the role that God played in the creation of America in their speech and writings:

It cannot be emphasized too strongly or too often that this great nation was founded, not by religionists, but by Christians; not on religions, but on the gospel of Jesus Christ. For this very reason peoples of other faiths have been afforded asylum, prosperity, and freedom of worship here.
—**Patrick Henry, *The Trumpet Voice of Freedom***

Suppose a nation in some distant region should take the Bible for their only law Book, and every member should regulate his conduct by the precepts there exhibited! Every member would be obliged in conscience, to temperance, frugality, and industry; to justice, kindness, and charity towards his fellow men; and piety, love, and reverence toward Almighty God . . . What a Eutopia, what a Paradise this region should be. —**John Adams, *One Nation Under God***

When I made a commitment to bring my faith with me every day, I discovered a linear equation: If you want more God in your life, you need to include Him in all aspects of your life. My relationship grew deeper and the blessings in life dramatically increased. Open the door to a deeper and more fulfilling relationship with God through your thoughts, words, and good works.

Faith-Forward Journey

Slowly and steadily, I became more comfortable sharing my connection to Christianity outside of church. I told friends and colleagues I was praying for them in a way that exuded kindness and caring. I expressed my gratitude for the Lord through prayer everywhere, from Starbucks to my girls' school functions. I even changed my cell phone voicemail message so that when I missed a call, people heard "I'm living the day the Lord has made, I'll call you back!" These may sound like small gestures, but they've had a tremendous impact on my life and my journey to CAVU. Becoming more vocal about my faith—praying with others, talking about Christ, having conversations about the Bible—wasn't about giving up personal desires and goals. I still wanted to achieve great things, but I wanted to reach my goals *while* working in concert with Christ. Sharing my Christianity openly kept my God connection flowing and helped me better see my moral horizon. It strengthened my faith in immeasurable ways, which helped me fight temptation in my life and helped inspire others to share their faith. These are some important evolutions of living faith forward.

Ignore Yourself

My opening daily prayer is about ignoring myself and fighting against my wants, desires, materialism, ego, and sinful ways. I fail every day, but I am not deterred from my ultimate goal to live a life for God and not for myself. I ask that God give me passion, energy, and perseverance to carry out His will in my life.

The more time you focus outside yourself, the more fulfilled you will be. Focus on your family, friends, and using your talents for *good*. Excessive pride will rob your life of happiness and create great unrest in your heart. To take the focus off of yourself, stop comparing yourself to others, be grateful for what you do have, don't worry about things you have no control over, and push aside everyday frustrations—accept them as part of God's plan for your life. Rise up each morning and commit your life to being a vessel for God.

The Book

Open the Bible for five minutes every day. For me, the simple act of opening the Bible brings instant comfort and peace. Dedicating just five minutes before I go to sleep to reading God's book is an intentional faith-forward act that I practice. It serves as an invitation to God to enter my life. If you are not religious or practicing, substitute the Bible for some words of wisdom from a philosopher—be open to challenging your perspective and beliefs.

The Power of Prayer

Eddie Murphy began his career on *Saturday Night Live* at age nineteen. He openly shares that his belief in Jesus and constant prayer has kept him from falling into the traps that snare so many young actors. Prayer can be soothing, a way to tap into your spirituality. It forces a greater connection to God and can keep you focused on your values and your pursuit of positive choices. Patrick Mahomes, the youngest MVP and quarterback to win the Super Bowl, is a spirit warrior. As part of his game preparation, he attends chapel on Saturday night, and on game day he walks the field and says a prayer. Armed with a faith-forward mentality, he asks the fans to pray for him so that he can play without fear and be himself on the field. Win or lose, Patrick's ultimate goal is glorifying God with his actions.

Perhaps the best thing about prayer is that you can do it anywhere. At home, traveling, or deployed—my prayer routine is the same regardless of my location. I love to combine prayer with my morning workouts. It is important to have a structure to your prayers; this allows you to make it repeatable and part of your routine. I have a rote list of prayer I follow that includes the areas that are most important in my life: my family, friends, health, work, and ambitions. I complete this every day, in addition to my running conversation with God. Prayer invites God into our lives in real ways. As is stated in Matthew 6:25, pray more and worry less— *faith kills fear.*

Be Present

Why are we always in a rush to the next thing—the next meeting, the next kids' event, the grocery store? We scurry about in constant motion, sprinting to the next event on our calendar. Be present in your interactions. Take a deep breath and don't worry so much about what's on the horizon. For the last thirteen years I have been the last one to leave virtually every event for Folds of Honor. I want to speak to everyone there, to connect with the people who cared enough to attend.

If someone has a question, I want to be there to answer it. I'm not thinking about everything else I need to do after, but rather I'm intentional about being present.

Give the Credit

Billy Mills is a fellow Jayhawk, a Marine, and a personal hero of mine. In the 1964 Olympics he won gold in the 10,000 meter, with one of the greatest comebacks in Olympic history. As a Native American, Mills had endured extreme poverty and racism as a child. His entire life had been thrust into the wind, but in the wake of his Olympic victory he credited his dad's advice to him: "Find your dream. It's the pursuit of that dream that heals broken souls." You may have worked hard to be the best fighter pilot, hit the winning shot, or close a big deal at work, but it is God who gave you the talents and desires to become everything in your life. When you receive praise—big or small—recognize that it is the perfect moment to say thank you by giving credit to the Lord and to your loved ones.

Be Blessed

It's a simple one I use: When people ask me how I am doing, I reply, "I am blessed. God is doing awesome things in my life." You would be amazed at the reactions. Whether I'm in the fighter squadron, playing golf, or walking through the airport, people stop in their tracks when I respond openly with my faith. Why? Because few are used to hearing how much God factors into life. We have stopped sharing our faith. Every time you share your faith, God enters your life.

Don't Pile On

My mom always said, if you don't have something good to say, don't say anything. This is especially true when it comes to talking about other people. Gossip is easy—to pile on when someone else is struggling, or to jump into a negative conversation, kicking people when they are down. I believe that is one of the gravest sins and worst examples of being faith forward.

Do your very best not to judge people—we never know the entire story or circumstance in the moment, and none of us know what the final judgment will look like. Being faith forward requires that you focus on yourself: make yourself better by avoiding parsimonious gossip.

Go Last

On Christmas Day 1998, General Charles Krulak, then commandant of the Marine Corps, made a stop before his family dinner to visit the Marines on duty at Quantico. When he arrived, he was dismayed that he could not find the officer on duty; rather, only a young enlisted Marine was present. General Krulak asked the young Marine for the name of the officer on duty. "Sir, it's Brigadier General Mattis," he said. Yes, that's right, one of the highest-ranking members of the Marine Corps had volunteered to serve on Christmas to allow the troops to be home with their young families.

Go last and put others in front of yourself. This is such an easy way to be faith forward. The simple act of saying "after you" and letting someone jump ahead of you in line at a coffee shop, or just allowing others to order before you when eating out with friends, sends a quick but powerful message. As does letting a colleague speak first at a meeting, even if you're anxious to jump in with your idea. Waiting is letting you (and the other person) know that you don't view yourself as more important. Deferring to someone else's needs is humbling and will help you see that the world does not revolve around you, your to-do list, and your deadlines.

When making an effort to bring more faith into your life, take a minute to think about how you can use your God-given talents to help others. While any service for others is positive (working at a soup kitchen, volunteering in a shelter, and so on), God has blessed you with unique gifts that are all your own. What skills do you possess, and how can you use them to be a vessel of God and make the world a better place?

Full-Time Faith

President Jimmy Carter, who, at ninety-five years old, still builds houses for Habitat for Humanity, teaches Sunday school, and is a Nobel Peace Prize recipient, puts it this way: "We should live our lives as though Christ were coming this afternoon." In other words, being a son of thunder is a full-time job; it's not something you turn on to impress people or pull out to feel good about yourself. My brother in Christ and great friend PGA Tour golfer Rickie Fowler writes scripture verses on the golf gloves that he gives to his young fans. What a powerful way to use his influence and share his faith. Staying in line with your moral horizon takes work and requires reflection, dedication, and determination. But most of all, it takes *faith*. Faith is about your belief in God, sure, but it's also about your belief in yourself. Faith is that wonderful expectation of good things to come, of knowing God loves you, and that your sense of purpose and direction will drive you forward.

Re-cage Your Spiritual Horizon

Our faith walk is a long journey, and if you are like me, you will occasionally end up in the milk bowl, spatially disoriented but morally committed to get reoriented to God. Below is my personal go-to list in order to re-cage my spiritual horizon. As you'll see, each of the seven deadly sins is listed below, matched next to its spiritual and moral opposite. If the milk bowl shows us anything, it's that if you're down, you're only a 180-degree turn from up:

- Pride versus humility

- Envy versus gratitude

- Greed versus generosity

- Anger versus patience

- Gluttony versus temperance

- Lust versus chastity

- Sloth versus diligence

10

Force Multiply

Colleagues share food. Wingmen share fate.
—**Indian Air Force advertisement**

The F-4 Phantom was a fighter pilot's jet: fast, robust, and powerful. And on March 10, 1967, two F-4s were part of a strike package fragged for the most difficult mission in the Vietnam air war to date. The target, thirty miles north of Hanoi, was a heavily defended steel mill that produced essential war materials. Modern-day fighter pilots still refer to a combat sortie as "going downtown," in recognition of the brave pilots who flew into the teeth of the tiger over Hanoi.

Captain Earl Aman (pilot), First Lieutenant Robert Houghton (back seat RIO⋆), Captain Robert Pardo (pilot), and First Lieutenant Steve Wayne (back seat RIO) knew that on this mission jets were almost certain to be shot down. Intelligence had briefed up the target area and noted a hornet's nest of antiaircraft artillery (AAA), surface-to-air missiles, and enemy MiGs.† When the strike package was eventually launched from Ubon Royal Thai Air Force Base, it hit a pre-strike air refueling tanker and ingressed directly to the target area. Seventy-five miles from Thai Nguyen, Aman and Houghton's jet began shaking violently. They had been hit by AAA, but thankfully the jet was still flyable and all gauges appeared in the green.

Most crews would have turned back to home plate, but Aman and Houghton decided that today was too important to jettison their six 750-pound bombs and leave their element lead, Pardo. The brave crew continued to press toward the high-value target. As Pardo and Aman approached the steel mill, the haunting sound of emergency beacons filled the radios from the Ameri-

---

⋆ Radar Intercept Officer.
† Russian fighter aircraft made by the Russian Aircraft Corporation MiG.

can pilots who had already been shot down. Both crews pressed through heavy enemy fire and successfully delivered their bombs on time on target. However, once they came off the bombing pass, both F-4s were hit by multiple rounds of AAA.

Aman and Houghton had the more pressing problem of the two planes, since their F-4 was losing fuel rapidly. They knew they didn't have enough gas to make it safely back to their base in Thailand, but if they ejected over the area they had just bombed, their fate was likely death or extreme torture in the infamous Hanoi Hilton.* Meanwhile, Pardo's emergency panel was lit up like a Christmas tree, indicating multiple system failures. He had lost electrical power and was leaking fuel, but miraculously his jet was still flying well. Pardo directed the formation to snap south and climb to 30,000 feet to save precious fuel. Aman copied and replied that they were preparing to bail out.

"Don't jump, we're going to do our damnedest to help you fly out of here," said Pardo.

In the problem-solving spirit most critical for a fighter pilot's livelihood, Pardo came up with a solu-

---

* The nickname of Hỏa Lò Prison, where the North Vietnamese kept U.S. prisoners of war.

tion to a dire situation: He radioed to Aman that he was going to fly underneath Aman's jet and attempt to push him. Pardo remembered the story of Robbie Risner, who used his F-86 to push his crippled wingman in Korea. With no other options, Pardo's first idea was to push the nose of his plane against the drag chute of Aman's plane, but that plan didn't work: The turbulence coming off of Aman's plane prevented Pardo from getting close enough to execute the maneuver.

Luckily, Pardo quickly came up with another idea. He had Aman drop the tailhook on the back of his F-4. At this point, Aman's plane was flying at 300 knots, dropping like a rock at 3,000 feet per minute, and was on fumes with a mere 400 pounds of fuel in the tank. Pardo acted fast and positioned Aman's tailhook on the metal canopy bow of his windscreen. The push worked, as Aman's speed of descent decreased by half, but Aman's motors, starved of fuel, soon flamed out. Pardo kept his jet in perfect formation and continued to push his wingman's 30,000-pound glider. Just when the situation could not get any worse, Pardo noticed a fire warning light and increasing EGT on his left engine. As such, he was forced to shut the #1 engine down or risk blowing up the formation.

Two jets, one engine, and swarming enemies below is not a good day at the office. As the planes' descent rate increased to 2,000 feet per minute—the mountains and trees were quickly getting bigger in the windscreen—Pardo got on the radio and informed search and rescue forces of their position just south of the Black River. It was time to give the jets back to the taxpayers.

Houghton and Aman ejected first, while Pardo and Wayne followed two minutes later. They had pushed Aman and Houghton fifty-eight miles (5 + 8 = 13), but they were all still over enemy territory. Every mile farther south provided precious time for the rescue helicopters. All four men sustained injuries during the ejection and were close to being captured. Thankfully, the heroes flying the A-1Es and Jolly Green Giant helicopters fought off the enemy and successfully rescued the crews. Pardo's heroic maneuver is legendary in the fighter-pilot world and became known as Pardo's Push. He risked his own life (as well as Steve Wayne's), but he knew that if Aman wasn't helped, he and Houghton would go down in the most dangerous part of Vietnam.

The valor of this act exemplified the best of the fighter-pilot world and some seriously brave problem solving. Furthermore, an unshakable bond was created between the men that day. Years later, when Aman was suffering from ALS, Pardo created the Earl Aman Foundation to buy him a voice synthesizer, computer, motorized wheelchair, and van. He was going to be Aman's wingman until the very end.

The concept of the wingman existed long before anyone ever heard of Maverick and Goose from the classic movie *Top Gun*. Though the ancient Romans didn't utilize wingmen the same way we do today, they did understand the importance of the wing position when it came to waging battle. Infantry was placed in the center, the cavalry on the wings. The cavalry's job was to prevent the infantry from being outflanked. For this method to work, both the infantrymen and the cavalry needed to understand their specific roles and execute them properly. This lethal combination made the Roman army dominant from AD 27 to 476.

The same principle that helped the Roman army conquer the world exists today in the U.S. Air Force. The wingman's main job is to support and provide protection for the flight lead's aircraft. While the flight lead and wingman share a common purpose when they fly, each plays a highly specific role essential to the success of any sortie or mission. Together, they form a lethal and cohesive team.

As we press on into the next LOE, we will discuss how you can adopt a wingman culture into your life. Building a life squadron will allow you to force multiply in powerful ways and persist with ultimate valor.

LOE #9: FORCE MULTIPLY

A study conducted by Harvard that began in 1938, and continues today—the world's longest study of the mental and physical well-being of adults—found that our close relationships are the biggest indicators of our health and happiness. The findings revealed that relationships, more than health, money, or fame, are what keep people happy throughout their lives. Those connections protect people from life's discontents, help to delay mental and physical decline, and are better predictors of long and happy lives than social class, IQ, or even genes. Human beings are social creatures. In order to thrive (and to *survive*), we require social contact. The American Association for the Advancement of Science showed that not having social connections is more detrimental to your health than obesity, high blood pressure, and even smoking.

While it's clearly important to make genuine connections, modern life doesn't feel set up to cultivate and nurture relationships outside of Facebook or Instagram. It seems more and more that any brief respites we get from our crazy ops tempo are spent descending into the virtual sludge of our mobile devices. It is hard to make relationships a priority, but being lucky enough to experience the unwavering support of wingmen, I know how beneficial these relationships can be.

The pilot-wingman relationship has shown me that to achieve success it is critical to "force multiply," the process by which "a capability, when added to and employed by a combat force, significantly increases the combat potential of that force and therefore enhances the probability of successful mission accomplishment." Simply put, your family, marriage, faith, friends, physical well-being, and professional success culminate to form your life mission, and for that mission to be successful, you can't do it alone. You have to surround yourself with people who support you and share your values. To force multiply and achieve CAVU, you need to build a life squadron. Of all the LOEs this book presents, force multiply is the one concerned most with happiness. (Don't forget to smile!)

Build Your Squadron

Air Force squadrons are operational units responsible for various duties. My current squadron is the 301st Fighter Squadron based out of Eglin AFB in the Florida Panhandle. Every airman within a squadron has an AFSC (Air Force Specialty Code), which describes one's specific job. The best loose comparison of my squadron's job is the Air Force version of Viper in *Top*

Gun, the senior ranking pilot who mentors Maverick, played by Tom Skerritt.

At Eglin, we have thirty exceptional pilots who replicate enemy fighters and tactics (China and Russia) against F-22 Raptors and various other fighters. Our objective is to deliver a threat-replication to challenge and ultimately make the pilots we train against more lethal. When the squadron lands after a large force exercise (forty-plus jets), we continue to support each other. Our wingman culture does not stop once we shut down our engines.

Keeping in line with the Air Force concept that we are *stronger together,* I have found that there is no problem or challenge my life squadron can't fight its way through. We all bring unique skills and fresh perspective to the table. The collective culture of our squadron is—*make it work.*

While I am fortunate to have a squadron of exceptional friends, great colleagues, five beautiful children, and nurturing parents, it is my wife who provides the greatest support in my life. Military spouses are this country's unsung heroes and our ultimate support mechanisms. Across this nation they are pulling the load—putting in hard work, devoting all of their energy toward staying positive and hopeful—but they don't receive a fraction of the credit they deserve. Military spouses are our nation's wingmen. They stay back protecting our most precious gifts—our children—so that our deployed military can do their job and keep our nation safe. If you're ever at the airport when deployed military are being welcomed home, or if you see a soldier in a restaurant eating with his family, yes— absolutely thank them for their service. But take a minute to also thank their spouse.

My wife, Jacqy, has devotedly cared for our five children and the needs of our household during my three combat deployments. In our twenty-one years of marriage, I have been physically gone half of that time. She has handled holidays, birthdays, milestones, illnesses, injuries, and mishaps all on her own. She's driven me to the base in the middle of the night, not really knowing what our future held but understanding that no matter what happened, she'd be the one to have to cope alone. Before a combat deployment, it is customary to write a letter to your spouse in the event you don't make it home. The following is the letter I wrote to Jacqy and gave to my commander, Lieutenant Colonel Scott "Otter" Stratton, to pass on if I didn't make it back from my third tour in Iraq. I share it with her permission, in the hope of providing some perspective on the sacrifice all military families are prepared to make in defense of our nation.

DATE: 5 SEPT 2008

DEAR JACQY,

AS I THOUGHT OF WHAT TO WRITE TO YOU IN THIS LETTER, I REMEMBERED AN ENCOUNTER WE HAD A FEW YEARS BACK. MOST PEOPLE WOULD CALL IT CHANCE, BUT YOU AND I BOTH KNOW THERE IS NO SUCH THING AS CHANCE.

I REMEMBERED AN EVENING WHEN WE TREKKED ON THE BANKS OF A COVE ALONG THE SHORE OF LAKE MICHIGAN. WE WERE HAVING A CONVERSATION ABOUT NOTHING, ONE OF MY FAVORITE THINGS TO DO WITH YOU, BY THE WAY, WHEN THAT OLD MAN EMERGED. HE HAD A SOFT SMILE ON HIS BROWN AND WEATHERED FACE. "I'VE BEEN WATCHING YOU," HE SAID. AS HE TURNED HIS GAZE TOWARD THE LAKE, I COULD SEE TEARS WELLING IN HIS EYES. HIS LIP QUIVERED. "MY WIFE PASSED AWAY TWO MONTHS AGO. I CAN SEE THE LOVE YOU HAVE FOR EACH OTHER, AND IT REMINDS ME OF THE LOVE MY WIFE AND I SHARED. WE SPENT FIFTY-SEVEN YEARS TOGETHER, AND NOW THE LORD HAS TAKEN HER FROM ME."

HE TURNED BACK TO US WITH A REMINDER: "LOVE EACH OTHER AND ENJOY EVERY MOMENT TOGETHER, BECAUSE IT SEEMS LIKE ONLY YESTERDAY THAT MY WIFE AND I WERE

WALKING ON THIS VERY BEACH, JUST LIKE YOU TWO, OUR WHOLE LIVES AHEAD OF US."

As I REMEMBERED THIS, JACQY, I THOUGHT ABOUT OUR LIVES . . . BOTH THE GOOD TIMES AND THE TIMES WE WERE TESTED. THEY WERE ALL PART OF THE JOURNEY AND PART OF WHAT MADE OUR COMMITMENT AND MARRIAGE SO STRONG.

IT SEEMED LIKE YESTERDAY THAT I FIRST SAW YOU AT THE SIGMA CHI HOUSE. YOU WERE SO DIFFERENT THAN ALL THE OTHER GIRLS. I HAD NEVER MET ANYONE WITH A SMILE SO INFECTIOUS. YOU WERE SO POSITIVE, AND YOU LAUGHED ALL THE TIME. WE NEVER STOPPED LAUGHING.

IF I HAVE ONE COMPLAINT, IT'S THAT TIME PASSES TOO QUICKLY WHEN WE ARE TOGETHER. I CAN'T BELIEVE IT HAS BEEN SEVENTEEN YEARS. I WISH I COULD HAVE FROZEN OUR LIVES IN TIME. OUR PARENTS ARE HEALTHY, THE KIDS ARE HAPPY, AND IN THEIR EYES WE ARE STILL THE COOLEST PEOPLE IN THE WORLD . . . AT LEAST FOR A COUPLE MORE YEARS ANYWAY.

THERE IS NO DOUBT THAT TOGETHER WE COULD GET THROUGH ANYTHING. YOU WERE MY FOUNDATION, ALWAYS THERE TO LEND A HAND OR ADVICE. THE MILK FOR MY LOW-FAT OREOS. MY MOTIVATION TO GET A LITTLE BIT BETTER EVERY DAY.

YOUR UNCONDITIONAL SUPPORT GAVE ME THE COURAGE TO DREAM BIG. REGARDLESS OF HOW DIFFICULT THE DAY, I ALWAYS

KNEW THAT IT WOULD BE ALL RIGHT WHEN I GOT HOME. AS I WALKED THROUGH THE FRONT DOOR, REGARDLESS OF HOW CRAZY THINGS WERE, YOU'D STOP AND TAKE FIVE SECONDS TO GIVE ME A KISS.

THANK YOU FOR BEING MY WIFE. THANK YOU FOR ALLOWING ME TO BE ME. THANK YOU FOR STEERING ME THROUGH THE DIFFICULT TIMES . . . YOU ALWAYS HAD JUST THE RIGHT WORDS, EVEN WHEN I WAS THE ONE BEING DIFFICULT. THANK YOU FOR WAKING UP HAPPY EVERY MORNING. THANK YOU FOR KEEPING ME YOUNG AND SHARING MY PASSION FOR LIFE.

IT WAS AMAZING HOW WE WERE ALWAYS ON THE SAME WAVELENGTH . . . ALTHOUGH YOU DO LIKE REALITY TV? I WAS NEVER ABLE TO UNDERSTAND THAT? YOU FIGURED OUT LIFE, AND I WAS PLAYING CATCH-UP WITH YOU FROM THE DAY WE MET. YOU NEVER LOST TOUCH WITH THE LITTLE KID IN YOU. YOU'RE ALWAYS GIGGLING . . . JUST THINKING OF YOUR LAUGH MAKES ME SMILE. I LOVED GIVING YOU PRESENTS BECAUSE YOU APPRECIATE EVEN THE TINIEST GESTURE. MOST OF ALL, I JUST ENJOY HANGING OUT WITH YOU. THE SIMPLEST MOMENTS CHILLING OUT IN THE EVENINGS, WATCHING THE KIDS PLAY IN THE DRIVEWAY. MY FAVORITE PLACE ON EARTH.

JACQY, YOU ARE AN AMAZING MOTHER. I WAS ALWAYS IN AWE WATCHING YOU TAKE CARE OF OUR LITTLE GIRLS. WHILE I HELPED, YOU WERE DOING MOST OF THE WORK, ENSURING THAT

OUR GIRLS HAD THE FOUNDATION FOR A GOOD LIFE. THEY ARE GROWING UP IN A SAFE AND POSITIVE ENVIRONMENT.

THE LAST FEW YEARS WORKING TOGETHER ON THE FOUNDATION WERE AWESOME. IT WAS WONDERFUL TO SHARE THE EXPERIENCE OF TRUE GIVING WITH YOU. I COULDN'T THINK OF A BETTER EXAMPLE TO SET FOR OUR CHILDREN OR A BETTER WAY TO GIVE BACK TO A COUNTRY THAT HAS GIVEN US SO MANY OPPORTUNITIES.

I WANT YOU TO KNOW THAT I CHECKED OUT DOING WHAT I LOVED TO DO. I WILL MISS YOU SO MUCH. I WILL MISS WAKING UP ON SATURDAY MORNINGS, WASHING THE CARS, AND WATCHING FOOTBALL TOGETHER. I MISS OUR LONG WALKS AND LAZY VACATIONS. I MISS OUR EXERCISE DATES . . . ISN'T IT FUNNY HOW OUR BEST TIMES DIDN'T COST ANYTHING?

PLEASE DON'T LET THE GIRLS FORGET THEIR DAD, AND TEACH THEM ABOUT ME AS THEY GET OLDER. KEEP THE LEGEND ALIVE OF THE ROLLER-COASTER MAN, FREEZE MONSTER, AND THE WOLF. LEAVE PICTURES OUT AND SHARE STORIES. PLEASE HAVE THEM PRAY FOR ME EVERY DAY. GIVE THEM HUGS AND KISSES FROM THEIR DAD. TELL THEM I SAID, "DREAM BIG!" TEACH THEM ABOUT VOLITION. CHALLENGE THEM TO USE THEIR TIME AND TALENTS TO POSITIVELY IMPACT THE WORLD. LET THEM KNOW HOW MUCH I LOVE THEM AND THAT I AM ALWAYS IN THEIR HEARTS. DURING THEIR TOUGHEST TIMES I WILL BE

THERE TO GIVE THEM STRENGTH. I WILL BE WITH THEM ON THEIR WEDDING DAYS.

ABOVE ALL ELSE, I WANT YOU TO BE HAPPY. NEVER STOP LAUGHING AND KEEP SMILING. YOUR HAPPINESS IS YOUR GREATEST BLESSING. KNOW THAT I WILL ALWAYS BE WITH YOU. YOU SAVED ME, AND I WILL BE WITH YOU TO RETURN THE FAVOR. I AM SO SORRY I WILL MISS THE REST OF THE JOURNEY. ALWAYS KNOW THAT I WILL BE IN YOUR HEART AND THAT I WILL BE WATCHING OVER YOU.

I LOVE YOU TO INFINITY.

—DAN

Standards and Evaluations

Standards and Evaluations is a department of a flying squadron comprising hand-selected pilots called SEFEs who administer check rides to all the pilots in the squadron. A check ride is a formal evaluation, and pilots receive a mission and instrument check every eighteen months to ensure that they are meeting the highest standards. Though it sounds harsh, having a standards and evaluations process to rate your relationships is necessary.

This is the most critical and difficult part of building your squadron. People form a multitude of friendships over the course of a lifetime, from childhood to high school to college to the workforce to random social gatherings. It's a blessing to know so many people from different aspects of your life. While I'm not suggesting that you have to trim your list of friends down to the top five, the bottom line is that some relationships give you nothing, others fuel you (they increase your sense of belonging and purpose), while, sadly, some burn you out.

It is a proven truth that your relationships have the greatest impact on your happiness and overall well-being. Good friends listen, push you to achieve your goals, and rejoice in your successes. Conversely, we all have friends who approach life from a place of negativity. These friends have a tendency to foster your unhealthy habits, take little jabs at you and others, and cut you down when you experience success. To achieve CAVU, it is necessary to evaluate your relationships and identify the people who can help you grow. Be disciplined about seeking out the right wingman in order to build the most efficient life squadron.

Fill your ranks with people who are willing to truly support the real you. Synchronicity will bring the right people into your life, like it has for me. My college roommate introduced me to my wife (they were dating before we were). And during a round of golf with President Bush, Gavin Hadden from Fox News came into my life; his friendship and support of Folds has been monumental. Then there's the time I literally flew with Jesus, because when I returned to the Air Force, a fellow pilot by the name of Jesus "Gono" Figueroa would become one of my closet friends. Think about your walk and of how synchronicity has brought important people into your life. Be open to these moments orchestrated by God. When God places these special relationships in your life, hold on tight.

We have so many different relationships that demand our daily attention, it can be easy to get sidetracked and lose priority about whom you should invest in. I've found it helpful to organize my relationships into three categories: levels 1, 2, and 3. This is not to sound judgmental but rather to help you prioritize whom you spend the precious gift of time with. Level 1 consists of "drive-by relationships," acquaintances or people whom you enjoy chatting with, but whom you don't feel especially close to. They are people you see at the park, in your neighborhood, or at the soccer game. Level 2 relationships represent the biggest and most diverse bucket in our lives. These individuals can be family, coworkers, good friends, parishioners at church, or acquaintances with whom you partake in recreational activities. The sheer size of this group is both a blessing and a challenge. Level 2 is full of awesome people, but you need to be mindful of potential imbalances with level 2 relationships that may prevent you from prioritizing level 3. I find that my calendar is an excellent deconfliction tool. I am very active in the level 2 realm from nine to five, but have grown particular in regard to how and with whom I spend my evenings and weekends. And I've decided that weekends are sanctuaries for my level 3 relationships. There are certainly exceptions for dinner with friends and for just having fun, but my weekends generally consist of staying home with family. I enjoy watching a movie, playing a round of golf with Dad, going on walks with my kids and the dogs, and making chocolate chippers. I also stow my mobile device and deploy the speed brakes so I can slow down and enjoy the stuff that really matters. Thus level 3 represents our deepest, most lasting relationships. These are the kinds of relationships you must invest in and nurture. Level 3 relationships consist of people who allow us to fully be ourselves; they love you when you are at the top of your game, and they're there for you when you're broken and in need of rebuilding. These are the relationships where you go *all in* and reciprocate the same kind of love that they espouse to you. Level 3 relationships include your spouse, children, close family, and closest friends. You must be watchful and attentive to these relationships at all times. They deserve and require care and feeding. Nothing in life is more important than your level 3 relationships.

Shock and Awe

The twelve disciples, our founding fathers, night one of the Gulf War (Desert Storm), the 1980 U.S. men's Olympic hockey team, the 1985 Chicago Bears, and the 2012 U.S. women's Olympic soccer team—when the right squadron comes together, the force multiplier effect explodes. These are *shock and awe* examples, but their esteemed principles of getting the right group together and moving mountains apply to our individual lives.

There is order and intentional preparation required to build your squadron that, if followed, will put you in a position to force multiply. My goals were (and remain) wanting to have a successful marriage and family, have deep, meaningful relationships, help others, leave a strong legacy, and have lots of fun along the way. I have been blessed with a few moments in my life where the force multiplier effect has had a shock and awe impact upon me.

Here is a recent example. In 2018, like many golf courses in America, the Grand Haven Golf Club was struggling to make it. My parents and I had been funding the shortfalls for several years and Dad was getting too old to keep running the place. We were at a crossroads, but since Grand Haven was the birthplace of Folds of Honor, my parents, Jacqy, and I felt a deep, personal connection to it.

One of the earliest lessons I learned in the military was never to present a problem without at least two solutions. As a family we worked together and came up with two potential solutions. The easiest and most obvious was to sell it to a developer and cash out. We didn't want to go that direction, but if the second idea failed, we would have no choice but to sell the course off as land for development. Our second idea was to approach the great Jack Nicklaus and see if he'd be willing to help. (Okay, admittedly, that one was way out there.)

I had the privilege of meeting Jack Nicklaus through my work at Folds of Honor. He had served as the honorary chairman for Patriot Golf Day, but despite my desire I never got the chance to know him well. He was always gracious and then moved on to the next engagement, and I got it—most of us don't get to be friends with a GOAT who has won twenty major championships. Jack was one of my boyhood heroes, but to him I was just another acquaintance . . . a level 1 relationship.

I was nervous on my flight down to Jupiter, Florida, as I prepared to present our idea to Jack and his long-time manager, Scott Tolley. I carefully crafted what I would say and chair-flew my presentation. When I arrived, I met Jack and Scott on the back porch of the Bear's Club. We shared a few pleasantries, but then my preparation went out the window: I went straight to a level 3 relationship, and in a heartfelt stream of emotion I shared the details of our struggle and was open about our financial situation and my deep desire to save this place. I confided in him how I wanted to do right by my parents who had always believed in me and give them the gift of preserving a legacy they would be proud of. I had already given my idea a name, American Dunes Golf Club. In my vision cast I explained that this special place would be a collaboration of like-minded patriots and that he, Jack Nicklaus, would be the flight lead and I his wingman. We would scrape the old Grand Haven Golf Club site and reimagine a new course that would forever stand as a tribute to our military and commemorate the birthplace of Folds of Honor. American Dunes would transcend golf and serve as a safe haven for veterans and their families to find rehabilitation through the recreation of the game.

Each day we would celebrate God, country, and our military without apology. Plus, 100 percent of American Dunes' annual profit would be given to the Folds of Honor Foundation.

When I was done with my emotional pitch, I took a deep breath. We sat in silence for a moment and I looked at Jack's steely blue eyes, with no idea of what his response would be. But like so many times before in my life, the Holy Spirit would connect us in a powerful way. Jack understood my heartfelt stream of consciousness, but he also followed up with several thoughtful questions before declaring, "I will go along with your crazy idea. I am all in!" Right there, he pledged to lend his name and to design American Dunes at no charge ($3 million is his usual design fee). In addition, he committed to help me share the story and round up a few of his friends to assist. Virtually all my level 3 relationships have come out of moments of adversity. Today was no different, and Jack, Barbara, and I were now real level 3 friends.

After our meeting, Jack, Scott, and I walked out of the clubhouse together under a fittingly CAVU sky. I celebrated that night in the Palm Beach airport with a cold Budweiser and gave thanks to God, but like any big idea, the process of bringing American Dunes to life would be full of gray and often turbulent conditions. We had permitting challenges, financial challenges, and our share of people who wanted us to fail.

As you well know by now, I firmly believe that when you are on the right path, God conspires for you. He did at American Dunes, and construction began in November 2018 on the site of the Grand Haven Golf Club. Situated a few hundred yards off Lake Michigan, tucked in majestic sand dunes, the original course cut through a massive forest, and most of the holes looked like bowling alleys, completely flanked by trees. Jack's design focused on removing thousands of trees and scraping the original site down to pure beach sand. It was a long transformation process, but one that symbolized the great reward of perseverance.

Jack uncovered a massive amphitheater of sand that rolled across the site like waves rolling across Lake Michigan. With a clean canvas, he brought the raw dunescape to life. His weathered hands sketched out each hole in precise detail. As I watched, I couldn't help but marvel at all the things those hands have accomplished in golf. Most days blend together and are forgotten, but this experience with Jack and my dad was a sacred gift that I will never forget (they both turned eighty the year American Dunes was born, in 2020).

Jack uncovered and shaped a world-class golf experience, but that is not what makes it unique. Our "why" is what separates American Dunes from any other course in the world. In Israel, it is a common practice to put a church on historic biblical sites to mark their significance and give believers a place of pilgrimage. Similarly, we built a different kind of church for golfers who love God and country. American Dunes stands proudly on the birthplace of Folds of Honor and pays tribute to Jack and Barbara Nicklaus's legacy of supporting the military. The course has a unique meaning beyond the physical routing. Each tee box honors a service member killed in action, whose family is also a Folds of Honor recipient, and alongside each Folds of Honor tribute is one of Jack's major championships. At 1300 each day, we pause for "Taps" and thirteen bells. Each bell toll pays tribute to one of the thirteen folds that bring the flag to its triangle shape. What's more, in the fighter-pilot squadron bar at American Dunes, a scale model of Pardo's Push hangs proudly: May it always remind our guests that with the right wingmen and a creative problem-solving spirit, anything in life is possible.

Pardo's Push: Ask for Help

Ask for help. This is the greatest force multiplier in your life.

There are wingmen within your life squadron flying in formation and ready to help, but here's the key: You have to ask them. I get it—I still struggle to find the courage and openness required to sincerely ask someone for help (and it's sad that some perceive it as a sign of weakness). To the contrary, asking for assistance requires confidence and sincerity. And because each squadron is cemented by an invisible bond of struggle, the wingmen in your group will understand your circumstances when the time comes.

My path in life has afforded me the gift of many great relationships with exceptional people. It's God's grace that has come to me through my work at Folds of Honor. Still, I joke that when anyone picks up the phone and hears my voice it's probably a safe bet that I am asking for their support on behalf of our Folds recipients.

To force multiply you have to ask for help. When I look back at my walk I see the faces of the amazing people who have helped me: Mom and Dad; USAF fighter pilot General Steve "Reno" Cortright; Brian Whitcomb at PGA America; President Bush 43; Steve Haworth, who helped with Folds during our most trying times; the partners at The Patriot, American Dunes, Volition America; and Steve Doocey from Fox

News, who helped me get my book proposal into the hands of my publisher. I came to these people humbly, in real need of their help. And when someone asks me for help, I return the favor. That is our shared duty when we are all part of God's squadron.

POW—Prisoner of War

Mental health is a major issue in society. One of my goals in writing *Fly Into the Wind* was to share my code of living with the sincere hope that it would help some of my brothers and sisters in the military who are struggling. In my role at Folds of Honor, we support many military families who have lost a loved one to suicide.

The consequences of war are far-reaching and extend beyond the battlefield. Desert Storm was the last conflict in which we had soldiers held as POWs, but today we have modern-day prisoners of war. Our veterans are being held captive by visible and invisible wounds. Suicide among veterans is at an all-time high, with 20 vets taking their own lives every single day. This number has increased in four out of the last five years, doubling between 2007 and 2017. That's 60,000 veterans dying by suicide in the last ten years. The fallout from twenty years of fighting in the Middle East has overwhelmed our Veterans Administration system.

The VA has some major deficiencies, but it was never built to handle millions of veterans suffering from the invisible wounds of traumatic brain injury and PTSD.

The wingman role is taken very seriously in the Air Force: In the air we put our lives in each other's hands. That relationship doesn't stop as soon as we touch down. The Air Force has dedicated tremendous resources to fight the battle against suicide. On that mission we have adopted the four pillars of a wingman, and we constantly remind each other of them in the air and on land: physical, emotional, spiritual, and social. These core components help us to remain resilient, healthy, and in control.

Physical Well-Being

While taking note of whether your wingman is eating, hydrating, or has suffered any injuries might be more relevant during combat, there's nothing wrong with asking your wingman for support (or providing it) when it comes to physical well-being. Exercising with a friend is a great way to stay healthy while spending time together. Having a strong support system while trying to make big lifestyle changes like quitting smoking, curbing excessive drinking, or losing weight can make the difference between success and failure. Good health is a foundational component of CAVU, and having a positive friend cheering you on while making big changes can be the difference between success and failure.

Emotional Well-Being

When it comes to flying, we need to make sure there's nothing distracting us. Emotions need to be kept in check so that we go into battle with focus. A good wingman will help your mind stay in the game so that you can enjoy success in your various pursuits. He'll listen to you carefully and provide honest feedback: A wingman isn't there to stroke your ego. He might talk you through tough business decisions, provide support during a difficult choice, give marriage advice, or just be someone with whom you can blow off steam. Wingmen come in various forms. My service dog, Bravo, was provided by K9s for Warriors as an ambassador for our partnership. K9s for Warriors is an amazing organization that rescues dogs from kill shelters and trains them as service dogs for our veterans. Their program is one of very few to show results in stemming suicides. Dog is "God" spelled backward. I get it and believe it.

Social Well-Being

It's hard to be away from family for long periods of time, but socializing with other pilots can help. A wingman makes sure you're not withdrawing and that you're interacting with others and maintaining healthy connections even in the most difficult circumstances. On my first deployment in Iraq I had the opportunity to host Robin Williams for the afternoon and show him the F-16. Robin was visiting Incirlik, Turkey, as part of a USO tour. When I dropped him off, he took time and asked me how I was doing and if he could help. Looking back, that moment has a deeper and tragic meaning. A good wingman is always watching for signs of distress, isolation being one of them. I understand the desire to withdraw and stay home, but maintaining social ties is crucial to CAVU. A good wingman will urge you to get up and get out. He might convince you to go to that party that sounds like too much trouble or join in for a night of cards or a round of golf. Your wingman is someone you love engaging in conversation with or are comfortable just hanging out with, even if that means sharing silence together.

11
Go Before You're Ready

Growing up, I watched my VHS tape of *Top Gun* so many times that several scenes in the movie were worn down and almost unviewable. And since there weren't any fighter jets at the local Stillwater municipal airport, that warped tape served as my primary motivation. Thirteen years and probably a thousand viewings later, I would find myself breathing the beautiful smell of JP-8 jet fuel on one of the best days of my life. My dream of flying solo in the F-16 was finally about to come true.

The Undergraduate Pilot Training program had been the most intense challenge of my life up to that point. With Sheppard Air Force Base in our rearview mirror, I soon arrived at Luke, and endured a month of academics and simulators. The next step was getting airborne, in which I had to successfully complete four rides with instructors in the F-16D model, a two-seat variant. After my fourth flight, my IP, call sign "Rock," smiled big and half-jokingly said, "Don't kill yourself" as he signed my grade sheet. He cleared me to go solo in sequence with the syllabus at the F-16 schoolhouse. Getting cleared solo was required to prevent ending up as just another washout.

When I stepped out of the crew van at Luke Air Force Base, a.k.a. Fighter Country USA, I couldn't believe this moment had arrived. I approached the jet with more excitement than nervousness. I was confident in my ability, but to be completely honest, I didn't know if I was ready. It didn't matter, because I was going whether I was ready or not. I strapped into the jet and taxied out to the runway. Once cleared for takeoff, I blasted into the CAVU sky and safely flew the F-16 for an hour, even bringing it back for a nice landing.

As I climbed down the ladder from my first solo ride, I was changed forever. I didn't fully grasp it in that moment, but I had been given a life-altering gift.

THE FINAL *LOE*: GO BEFORE YOU ARE READY

"Go before you are ready" is the most powerful LOE, and incorporating this ethos will change you in unimaginable ways. I purposely placed this as the last evolution because it is the trigger to launch you into a life of CAVU. If you want to go big, you must go before you are ready. The great people and moments described in this chapter are connected by their virtues of defiance, and each offers a powerful example of what can happen when you go before you are ready. The stories herein share demonstrations of greatness, strength, and the courage required to jump with both feet and burn the boats because, well, there ain't no going back!

Find Your Inner Maverick

The first time I sat alone in the F-16, I wasn't completely sure I was up to the task of flying solo. But there I was, strapped in a $30 million jet that had a capability of flying Mach 2.1. Having flown just those four times before *and* with an instructor, everything I had studied and practiced in preparation for this moment didn't feel like enough. I took a breath, said a quick prayer, reached over with my left hand, and moved the JFS*
to start 2. That's right, no keys required to start the F-16—just a lot of faith. I understood at that moment that I had to push aside fear and focus on faith. I knew that my instructors believed in me enough to clear me

---

* Jet fuel starter.

to go solo and that I had been working toward this moment in one way or another my entire life. I sat at the end of the runway for just a few extra seconds, soaking in the moment. Then, I moved the throttle over the detent to full afterburner.

There is no really good way to describe what it is like to fly a fighter jet. Imagine playing football, a musical instrument, and *Call of Duty* all at the same time, while solving a sudoku puzzle and traveling at supersonic speeds. This crazy concoction comes together and forms a purely euphoric state. *Top Gun,* Hollywood's best depiction of the fighter pilot's office, isn't even close to the real thing, but in some bizarre way Tom Cruise and I were kindred spirits that day I flew over the Arizona desert. You see, Maverick may be a fictitious movie character, but I can attest to the fact that Tom Cruise is a *real-life* maverick. Growing up, Tom was a nomad, as his parents were constantly on the move (he attended fifteen different schools by the age of fourteen). Always a spiritual person, Cruise initially wanted to become a priest before discovering acting. His go-before-you're-ready moment occurred at eighteen when he dropped out of school and headed to New York City. Five years later, he was starring in the movie that changed my life.

Shoot the Moon

Great successes often occur before people feel they are truly ready for them. In 1970, a high school dropout in England named Richard Branson started a magazine with one of his buddies, called *Student*. This independent venture went so well that he soon managed to open a brick-and-mortar record shop with the profits. Fast forward just a couple of years and he pushed his success even further with the creation of his own record label and recording studio that he rented out to musicians in the area. The first album the company released went on to sell five million copies—not bad for a kid with no higher education, money, or experience. With a little spending cash in his pocket, Branson, now in his twenties, headed on vacation to the Virgin Islands. He was excited to meet up with a girl, but the flight he was taking was canceled due to mechanical problems (my priest calls this an "*O Felix Culpa*"—a "happy fault moment of intervention"). While Branson's previous ventures had been successful, at this time no one had ever heard of him and he wasn't making loads of money—*yet*. This did not stop him from taking a big step that he wasn't ready for. Branson chartered a private jet even though he technically didn't have the money to pay for it. He made a sign that simply said, "Virgin Air, all seats $29.00," and quickly filled up his new rental, made back all of his money, and got to his destination (with a lot of other happy passengers from the canceled flight). Branson would go on to found Virgin Airlines and become a billionaire several times over. His quest continues to shoot the moon, literally, as the driving force behind Virgin Galactic, which is working with NASA to make civilian spaceflight possible in the very near future. Both Branson and NASA have a long history of "go before you're ready."

The world knows the story of Apollo 11 and Neil Armstrong setting foot on the moon, but NASA's defining go-before-you're-ready moment actually occurred with the launch of Apollo 8, which was scheduled to be the first crewed flight of the Saturn V rocket. However, there was a big problem—Saturn V wasn't even close to ready. One test of the rocket had gone well, but the most recent test had gone terribly wrong. While NASA worked around the clock to prepare for the launch, they were faced with extreme scrutiny after the recent deaths of Gus Grissom, Ed White, and Roger Chaffee (a faulty wire had caused the pure oxygen in the command model to catch fire, killing all three astronauts). Amid congressional hearings and a public outcry to cancel the space program, George Low, manager of the Apollo program, never flinched. In fact, he made a momentous decision. With Christmas approaching, he reached out to the three astronauts William Anders, James Lovell, and Frank Borman, and told them to cancel their holiday plans; they'd be headed to the moon on Apollo 8 to attempt the first lunar orbit. Low compartmentalized the distractions and stayed focused on the task at hand. The lives of the Apollo 8 astronauts and the entire future of NASA depended on whether the Saturn V issues had been fixed.

The stakes couldn't have been any higher, and the decision to launch was made for December 23, 1968. Thanks to some exceptional problem solving by NASA engineers, and by God's grace, the Saturn V worked. Apollo 8 shot the moon and completed the first lunar orbit, which paved the way for Apollo 11, the first successful moon landing. En route to the moon on Christmas Eve, the astronauts broadcast live to the world's largest television audience in history and recited chapters 1–10 from the book of Genesis.

William Anders

We are now approaching lunar sunrise, and for all the people back on Earth, the crew of Apollo 8 has a message that we would like to send to you.

*In the beginning God created the heavens and
the earth.*

*And the earth was without form, and void;
and darkness was upon the face of the deep. And
the Spirit of God moved upon the face of the
waters.*

*And God said, Let there be light: and there was
light.*

*And God saw the light, that it was good: and
God divided the light from the darkness.*

James Lovell

*And God called the light Day, and the darkness he
called Night. And the evening and the morning
were the first day.*

*And God said, Let there be a firmament in the
midst of the waters, and let it divide the waters
from the waters.*

*And God made the firmament, and divided the
waters which were under the firmament from the
waters which were above the firmament: and it
was so.*

*And God called the firmament Heaven.
And the evening and the morning were the
second day.*

Frank Borman

And God said, Let the waters under the heaven be gathered together unto one place, and let the dry land appear: and it was so.

And God called the dry land Earth; and the gathering together of the waters called the Seas: and God saw that it was good.

And from the crew of Apollo 8, we close with good night, good luck, a Merry Christmas— and God bless all of you, all of you on the good Earth.

Paralysis by Analysis

While it certainly seems reasonable to get most of your ducks in a row before attempting something big (or dangerous, like flying a jet at the speed of sound), most people tend to overanalyze their given situations. Ready, aim . . . aim . . . aim . . . aim. Our unreasonable perception of what "ready" really is prevents us from actually firing.

There's a big difference between being mentally and physically prepared and having it all perfectly analyzed. Perfectionism can be the poison that infects our lives, dreams, and goals, and it can act like a weight that prevents us from taking any action at all. Break free from these insidious and debilitating mental roadblocks:

- **Vulnerability:** It can be frightening to think you might be judged by peers, lose control, or even fail. But if you play it safe, you can neither lose nor win.

- **Exclusion:** You might fear that if you don't perform perfectly, you won't belong and won't be accepted by a group. You'll be left out.

- **Shame:** Any flaws or mistakes will result in a feeling of great shame. This might be self-shame, or the shame of your family or colleagues.

- **Confusing perfection and excellence:** Hard work, dedication, talent, and practice should result in excellence—not necessarily perfection. Don't confuse the two.

Here and Gone

When Folds of Honor was young and I was working to get corporate sponsors, I thought about how great it would be to have Budweiser on board. After all, it was the beer that Maverick drank in *Top Gun*. At the time, I was still working out of a tiny room above my garage in Oklahoma and didn't have an office or a staff. Most glaringly, I was aware that my little operation might not seem very impressive to the folks at a major corporation like Anheuser-Busch. But my faith exceeded my fear. I told myself, so what if I was working above my garage? Our mission was strong, and I knew that we would ultimately be able to help thousands of military families. If I wanted Folds to thrive, I had to find the courage to face the very real possibility of rejection.

I jumped on a Southwest flight from Tulsa to St. Louis and drove my rental car to the brewery. I was not prepared for what I witnessed: Suffice it to say that August Busch built a cathedral to beer. My visit that day was a great field trip, but it was clear that the Budweiser Clydesdales were not going to saddle up with Folds of Honor in any significant way. Obviously, that wasn't the result I had hoped for, but I know our lives are defined every day by what we do when life doesn't go our way. My passion outweighed any negative feelings I had about being rejected, and I still harbored the belief and conviction that Budweiser was a perfect match for Folds . . . even if we weren't big enough for them, yet.

As Folds continued to grow, I kept making the pilgrimage to the brewery. I flew up every six months for the next three years, but still had little success. Then a tragic moment of synchronicity brought me back to St. Louis: A young soldier who was killed in Iraq also happened to be the son of the president's executive administrator, Sue Marler. This occurrence, terrible as it was, eventually led to a meeting with the company's president, Dave Peacock. I was set to fly up the morning of September 8, but a family emergency forced me to miss the only flight from Tulsa. I called Dave's office to reschedule, but he was booked for weeks. I knew this was a defining moment, one I'd probably not see again, so I used my personal credit card to charter a plane. With an empty private jet, and the gravity of the situation weighing on me, I called my dad to ride along for the meeting. We flew up and shared the Folds of Honor story.

When we finished the meeting, I will never forget what Dave said: "I make it a best practice not to get in the way of God's will; we will figure out a way to help Folds of Honor." True to his word, Budweiser stepped up and has since donated over $18 million in the last eight years. They are indeed "The Great American Lager," and their donation has fueled the educational dreams of more than thirty-four hundred deserving military families.

The bottom line is that we are all here and gone in a short period of time. When you feel called, don't ignore it. Dreams will die if they are not nurtured. It is incredibly easy to wait for a magical moment of readiness to come before any action is taken. People often use excuses to justify their fear—"I'll approach that client when my company is more established," or "Next year I am going to move away from these brutal winters and restart my life in a coastal town"—but time reminds us that there is no such thing as a perfect moment. If you spend your life in a holding pattern, the cost will be high. Your dreams just might freeze over and never have a chance of being realized. You will never rise up in God's intended light.

Godspeed

I finish all my emails and letters with the closing "Godspeed." By definition, it is a blessing for a prosperous journey. NASA bid John Glenn Godspeed before he piloted Friendship 7 and became the first man to orbit the earth. I love the term because it combines purpose (God) with motion (speed). I strive to always live my life with both. Your idea is meaningless if your fears keep you from putting it into motion. My golf coach at Kansas, Ross Randall, gave me some incredible advice:

"Try your ass off, but don't give a damn what happens."

Failure Is Not an Ending

Our lives are defined by what we do when things don't go our way. If there is a single lesson to take away from failure, it is how rare individuals embrace it and channel it as motivation. For example, the late Kobe Bryant, Lakers star and NBA legend, became one of the best NBA players in history and a powerful hero to so many due to his never giving in to failure.

> When you make a choice and say, "Come hell or high water, I am going to be this," then you should not be surprised when you are that. It should not be something that is intoxicating or out of character because you have seen this moment for so long that . . . when that moment comes, of course it is here because it has been here the whole time, because it has been [in your mind] the whole time. **—Kobe Bryant**

At the end of his rookie season, while playing in game five of the Western Conference semifinals against the Utah Jazz, Kobe shot an air ball in the final seconds of regulation. The game went into overtime, and in the final minute of the period, Kobe added three more air balls, solidifying the end of the Lakers' season. This could have been a crushing moment, but not for Kobe. The Lakers flew back to LA, his teammates went home to bed, but Kobe went to a local high school gym and shot baskets all night and into the morning . . . *Mamba!* Kobe reminds us that our success is often about choice: We choose to be crushed by our failures or to channel them as motivation.

A guy I've known since high school embodies the same spirit as Kobe, only his special craft is music. I first encountered Garth Brooks at Oklahoma State University (to this day he still refers to his native Oklahoma as "the land of common sense"). Garth would hang around the geography department where my dad was chair. On the side, he was getting his music career started at a dive bar called Willie's on the strip.

Garth was a staple at Willie's. After he had played there for a few years, his friends lent him $600 to send him off to Nashville to try to make it "big" in the music business. When he arrived in town, he expected it to look like Cowboy USA, only to find it was mostly a suit-and-tie kind of place. Breaking into the country music industry wasn't at all going to go the way he thought it would. Scared, he admitted later, he turned around and went right back home. He spent less than twenty-four hours in Nashville, and he was so embarrassed that after he came back, he hid out at his parents' house in Yukon.

Eventually, Garth headed back to Stillwater, where he was surprised with unconditional support. This lifted his spirits and confidence to march forward. He soon married his college sweetheart, Sandy, and decided to give Nashville another good ol' country try.

Their restart was humble, and music didn't come close to paying the bills. Garth and Sandy were selling boots on the side to make ends meet. One day, Garth was hanging out at Bluebird, a well-known haunt for songwriters, when a man named Tony Arata sang an original song called "The Dance" (which Garth would later make famous). Garth loved the message in the song and felt that this moment was a whisper from God to keep persisting in the music business. He stayed the course, but still found it was a brutal progression of failure. He was turned down by seven different record companies, which, once again, reinforced his doubts about himself and the business. That would soon all turn around, however.

On a fateful night at the Bluebird, Garth was playing, slated to go on seventh. But he always showed up early. When an up-and-comer whom several music executives were in attendance to see didn't show, Garth was given that musician's spot. After he performed (game-changing synchronicity), an executive from Capitol Records who had turned him down earlier that day approached him. "We might have missed something. Let's talk," the executive said.

Garth would go on to be the number-one-selling solo artist in U.S. history, and "The Dance" would become his all-time biggest hit. Its lyrics remind us all that a failure does not mean the end: *Our lives are better left to chance / I could have missed the pain / But I'd have to miss the dance.*

12
Field Forward

My first mission after graduating from RTU at Luke was to enforce the no-fly zone (NFZ) in northern Iraq, which had been established to protect the Kurds from Iraqi forces post–Gulf War.

It is very rare to deploy so quickly out of training—heck, there are fighter pilots who will never deploy. Looking back, I can't help but chuckle at the thought of how unprepared I was for combat.

In the business, we call young wingmen "all thrust and no vector," which translated means "I was full of confidence but lacked the experience to back it up." Combat is a very challenging arena, especially for a young wingman. Every night before my combat missions, I lay awake and prayed that God would keep me safe and prevent me from making any stupid mistakes.

We called Iraq a banker's war because we fought from nine to five, Monday through Friday. Our jets took off the same time every day from Incirlik and pushed over the border into the lawless NFZ, where Saddam Hussein was always ready with a warm welcome, shooting AAA and launching surface-to-air missiles. It was early in my deployment, I was number four in a four-ship formation of F-16s when my flight lead, Steve "Robo" Kopp, came over the victor radio:

Padre flight push green 8 . . . Padre check—2, 3, 4.

The green frequencies are secure channels to keep the enemy from listening in, but they also make it difficult for us to hear. It sounded like a radio station that was just out of range. As I strained to listen, the controller explained that there was a rules of engagement (ROE) trip and we were being targeted for a retaliatory strike on an AAA compound on the outskirts of Mosul. Mosul is approximately four hundred miles north of Baghdad on the Tigris River. I remembered one thing very clearly from our intelligence briefings: Mosul had a huge red no-fly ring on the map that denoted it as one of the most heavily defended cities in all of Iraq. My heart started to race. *This should be interesting*, I thought.

We were given a 9-line over the radio, which is the

standard format we use during close air support and includes all the important information about the target area. The 9-line highlights are latitude and longitude coordinates, elevations, threats, and clearance to drop. As the controller's voice on the other side of the radio went through the 9-line, my brain lit off into the biggest helmet fire of my life. With all of the information running together, I was only able to pick up half of it, but luckily Robo—a Weapons School graduate and instructor—copied the firehose of information without missing a digit. Slowly, I relaxed a bit and was able to copy down what I had missed when Robo gave the mandatory readback. This redundancy was critical to ensure that there were no mistakes targeting the AAA compound. With the coordinates typed into the F-16 up-front control, the green pointer in our HUD swung almost straight south for a hundred miles near the 36th parallel over Mosul. As we pressed on a 185 heading, I worked feverishly, going through my weapons pages on the stores management system (SMS) while calibrating my targeting pod. I hit cursor zero three times on my targeting pod screen to take out any inadvertent INS slews. As we approached the target area, Robo came over the VHF radio: *You boys ready to drop?* Two months earlier, I had been in the O-club (officers' club) at Luke with my classmates enjoying some cold Budweiser and playing CRUD.* Was I ready?

Looking south, we could see the humidity of the Tigris River was spoiling our CAVU day, with the dusty brown desert reaching up and forming a blurry horizon against the blue sky that was filled with little white cumulus clouds. Where I grew up on the golf course in Oklahoma, those white puffies were a welcome friend on scorching summer days over the Stillwater Country Club, but when dropping laser-guided bombs, they are the enemy. You see, for the GBU-500 bomb to properly guide, it must follow the laser designation from our targeting pod. If the laser hits a cloud it will refract, and the seeker-head in the bomb will stop guiding, or "go stupid," in flight.

As we rapidly approached the target area, I looked at the eight-inch green monochrome screen over my left knee. The targeting pod's powerful camera allowed me to visually acquire and positively ID the target. As I began to break out details of my dimpi,† Robo cleared our two-ship to drag back into a ten-mile trail. Over the radio, he briefed that his two-ship would roll in and

---

* Full-contact pool game played by fighter pilots.
† Specific target.

drop first and that we would follow behind them and hit our targets.

We descended to the block 18,000–20,000 feet once we were twenty-five miles from the target. The sky immediately started to turn a grayish black. A voice over the radio warned us of possible AAA,* but we didn't need their heads-up. From the unrestricted view of my bubble canopy, the skies look liked a scene from one of my favorite boyhood movies, *Twelve O'Clock High*. Flak was exploding all around us.

Padre flight "cleared hot."

These are certainly the favorite two words of any fighter pilot. Translated, it means that we were cleared to go kinetic on the enemy that was trying to kill us. About the time my fangs started to come out, Robo announced that he was coming off dry due to clouds obscuring the target area. As we pressed in behind him, we saw that we faced the same situation. Blessed with incredibly high situational awareness, Robo looked south of the target and saw what appeared to be a clearer axis for the attack. At this point, the sky looked ablaze, and the mission commander on the radio was recommending a possible abort due to high threat of

---

* 120mm antiaircraft fire.

getting shot down. Robo ignored the commander and, without hesitation, swung the formation south, and a clear axis to the target opened up. *Contact, capture I reported over the radio. This is C3 comm letting the flight know that I have my target and am ready to engage. Green 'em up, the final command to master arm which energizes the release mechanism on the bombs.*

My jet was flying at 465 knots, but it felt like it was standing still. Everything was in slow motion. I TMS'ed* left on the stick to lock on to a huge AAA gun protected by a large revetment. I stared at the screen to confirm I had the correct sort with my flight lead and was locked to the proper target.

Master arm switch hot.

My focus moved to the HUD as the release cue marched down, Padre 4 bombs away. The jet shook violently as 500 pounds of the president's mail departed my jet.

Twenty-five seconds to impact.

I checked the jet 15 degrees left instead of the normal 30 degrees because of cloud formations that could obstruct the laser. I glanced outside and it looked like a sea of salt and pepper with all the black AAA mixed into the clouds.

---

* Threat management switched.

Fifteen seconds to impact—trigger on to ensure that laser is firing. Five, four, three, two, one.

There was a slight delay, a quick line-of-sight flash as the bomb flew through the targeting pod field of view. *Shack!* All hell broke loose as the scorching heat from tritonal inside the bomb fragged the gun and everything around it to pieces. Debris hurtled through the air and what was left of the pieces came slamming back to earth.

Padre—green north.

We lit the afterburners and stood the Vipers on their tails to get out of the AAA threat. With the extended time in the target area, we got a snap directly to the tankers since we were in need of gas. As I climbed through FL310 (31,000 feet), I dropped my mask and watched as water poured out. In the heat of the battle, I hadn't realized the intensity of the pressure, but now my flight suit looked like I had jumped in a pool, dark green and soaked with sweat. I looked out at the CAVU skies to the north and said a prayer of thanks that I was alive, as well as a prayer for the enemies on the ground.

After we landed back in Incirlik from our mission over Iraq, the intelligence team informed us during our debrief that our formation had been shot at over three hundred times. On that day I clutched my Saint

Michael medal that I wore around my neck (I still wear it) and cited this prayer upon hearing this news: *Saint Michael, defend us in battle, protect us against the wickedness and snares of the devil.* I took a deep breath: I had survived to fight another day.

Whether in combat or daily life, we need protection. As you launch on your quest to CAVU, beware of fear, doubt, and the people placed in your life who will keep you from your objective.

REGRET NOT

I wish I had the courage to live a life true to myself and not the life others expected from me.

That is the number one regret on people's death-beds, and it isn't surprising why. We spend so much time trying to appease others that we lose sight of our own dreams and passions.

Twenty-one years into my military career, I have few regrets. And on the jagged edges of a fast, uncompromising business, I have had the honor of working with amazing patriots. In some cases, I have seen them flourish from the battlefield into civilian life, and in others have witnessed the pain of too many lives cut short and the sadness in the faces of the families they have left behind. However triumphant or tragic the story, each patriot has given me the tools to learn how to lead, and, just as important, how to follow.

Every fighter pilot dreads the day of their fini-flight, but the day will come when I will move the throttle back and shut down those jet engines for the last time. I will climb down the ladder from a sortie and listen to the jet whisper back a beautiful sound as the fan blades slowly wind down—*clink, clink, clink*—to an eventual stop.

Our walk on earth is winding down each and every day—that is the beautiful irony of living. Make the most out of life by letting go of regret and being uniquely yourself. You'll find that the journey will feel longer, more rewarding, and spiritually boundless.

GOD IS REAL

One evening, after a meeting with Budweiser, I was in East St. Louis running down a gravel path adjacent to the Mississippi River, surrounded by an industrial wasteland with abandoned factories and graffiti-laden walls. The winter mist had turned into a steady, cold rain. My iPod died, and with it my motivation; my run slowed to a walk. I looked around and it was clear that I was all alone. It was a difficult time, as I had just quit flying the F-16 and was in the middle of my life storm. I felt like I had nothing left. I said a prayer: *God, please give me a sign that You are with me and that I am on the right path.*

Almost instantly, an American bald eagle appeared out of the overcast, its yellow eyes in sharp contrast to its dirty body. The bird's feathers mirrored the dingy brown color of the Mississippi's muddy waters. The eagle circled me three times in close proximity, then screeched as it disappeared in the rain. I felt a deep chill, not from driving rain but from the Holy Spirit. I knew that this was indeed a miraculous answer from God.

A moment of synchronicity would further affirm this sign when I returned a call later that evening to Ginger Gilbert. She is the widow of F-16 pilot Troy Gilbert, who was killed in Iraq, and their five children are Folds of Honor recipients. As I eagerly shared my God encounter, she listened and explained that today was Troy's birthday and that his favorite scripture was Isaiah 40:30–31: *Even youths grow tired and weary, and young men stumble and fall; but those who hope in the Lord will renew their strength. They will soar on wings like eagles.*

I walked onto my Southwest Airlines flight and headed home, renewed and confident that God is always with us, especially in our darkest times.

FIELD FORWARD

In the military we wear the American flag in what appears to be a backward position on the right sleeve. We call this *field forward,* and it represents the flag flying behind us as we move confidently into battle. A fighter jet takes off into the wind. Our lives, like a jet, need resistance and challenge to climb to the heights that God desires for us all. Understand that there will be resistance as you start the process toward CAVU. Press through it. Stop talking about it at Starbucks with your buddy. Go and do it. Whatever it takes. The smallest step creates momentum. I have been testing and proving that theory in my own life for forty-seven years. Build your own life. Create your own job description. I promise it will work out, just not in the way you probably envision. It's the universal truth.

PERFECTLY BROKEN

On graduation day you receive your first set of perfectly polished silver Air Force wings, you immediately break them. You give one half to your most trusted friend and keep the other. As a sign of humility and respect. Those wings will never come together until the end of your career. Eight years after my pilot training graduation, in

2008, Air Force One landed at Tinker Air Force Base in Oklahoma City. It was one of the greatest honors in my life to render a salute to my commander in chief just two weeks before I would deploy to Iraq. As we stood next to Air Force One, President Bush presented me the Call to Service Award and reminded me of those sacred words: *To whom much is given, much will be required.* While I have never been afraid to dream big, I never imagined the life-transforming storm waiting for me when I returned from Iraq. But it is in this brokenness that I would discover my true talents.

In Matthew 25:14–30, Jesus uses the parable of the talents. To make a long story short (though you should certainly read the long version), a rich man is going out of town and gives each of his three slaves a sum of money. The first is given five "talents," the second is given two, and the third is given one. They are left with instructions to care for the money. The first two servants use the talents to trade and make a profit, while the third is fearful and hides the one talent entrusted to him. When the master returns, he is delighted to see that the first two servants have doubled their talents, yet he admonishes the third for not investing the money and just hiding it away. The purpose of this story is to show us that God intends us to use our talents (whatever they may be) with reckless faith. Our God-given talents are not something to be hidden away and wasted; they are to be used!

I worked hard to learn to fly fighters and play golf at a high level: I accept that this is in part due to talent (but also to grit and perseverance). God shined a light on my other talents when Corporal Brock Bucklin's family came into my life. I learned from that experience that I have a talent to unite people for a greater good and spread the message of CAVU in my writing and speeches. I believe that being perfectly broken has fostered a genuine connection with people. So often we don't see what we are truly capable of until we are down and are forced to use skills we didn't know we had. Our break becomes an integral part of who we are as people. Without the darkness, I never would have discovered the bright steel-blue light of CAVU.

In Japan, brokenness is celebrated in a technique called *kintsugi*, or "golden joinery." When pottery is broken it is repaired with gold to highlight the points where the breakage occurred. The breakage, and subsequent repair, becomes part of the object's history—not something that is to be disguised. The next time you find yourself broken, know that you may be facing the opportunity to connect to your true God-given talent.

Give yourself credit when you turn dark corners and make it back into the light—*you've earned it.* There's a good chance that whatever trait you tapped into to get yourself to a better place can be used to do bigger things. Share your story and don't hide behind your vulnerabilities; they're an important part of your personal history.

By reason of breakings they purify themselves.
(Job 41:25)

It is time for you to move into battle, but not as you were before. You can never fully prepare for the unexpected, but that doesn't mean you're not capable of rising to the challenge. Now you are empowered with a code of living. You are armed with CAVU.

Follow the path of CAVU by using the LOEs and placing them in the proper order. Each evolution will move you bravely toward your quintessence. This mission is supposed to be hard, and it occasionally will hurt, but discomfort is a catalyst to progress. It is time for your new beginning. Listen to the unrest in your heart and make positive, sustained changes. Become a vessel of impact and leave it better than you found it.

Godspeed,

13

Epilogue: New Beginnings

When I was a twelve-year-old boy with an unlimited passion to chase my dreams, I couldn't have comprehended the direction my life would be headed twenty-six years later when, on one of the darkest days of my life, I walked away from that dream and a promising career as an F-16 fighter pilot. I never imagined my life circumstances would require me to stop flying and quit my military career short of twenty years. Needless to say, not all dreams go as planned.

Four years later, I would receive one of the greatest gifts of my life when Colonel Brian "Jethro" Neil put me back in the cockpit (in golf terms, he gave me a mulligan). It was a second chance to finish my military career and fly fighters again. I would soon discover that God had put Jethro and me together for a multitude of reasons: Colonel Neil was an amazing leader and brother in Christ who inspired me to become a better fighter pilot, family man, and person of faith. In addition to his inspiring me, Neil has become a mentor to so many other pilots. He has flown the T-38, F-16, F-22, and B-2, and along the way beaten cancer. He is an icon in our fast-jet business. It is my honor to share a little-known but amazing story about one of our great warriors, whom I am blessed to call my friend.

On September 11, 2001, America was attacked. Three days later, President George W. Bush told first responders, "I can hear you, the rest of the world hears you, and the people who knocked these buildings down will hear all of us soon." While President Bush and Congress were preparing to bring justice to our enemies, the B-2 stealth bombers were placed on high alert in preparation for a mission.

The B-2 is not a typical plane; it is the most expensive aircraft in the world, with a cost of $1 billion per jet. All of the twenty-one stealth bombers ever built are based in central Missouri at Whiteman Air Force Base. The B-2 made its combat debut in Yugoslavia during Operation Allied Force, but it was now warming up for its next mission in retaliation for the attacks on 9/11.

That's where then-captain Brian "Jethro" Neil comes in. He and Major Mel Deaile arrived at the heavily guarded entrance of Whiteman AFB on the cool, crisp night of October 7, 2001. The mission planners informed them that they would be the mission commanders for the second night of initial attacks on terrorist targets in Afghanistan. They stepped to the jet—bearing a prophetic name, "The Spirit of America"—and departed at 0200 to Afghanistan. Due to security reasons, the decision was made to fly west across the Pacific Ocean. The initial flight would last twenty-four hours and require five in-flight refueling sessions and deviations to avoid a typhoon. You are probably thinking, and rightly so, how does one stay awake? Usually, during noncritical phases of flight, B-2 pilots can grab some rest on a makeshift cot behind the ejection seats when they are not refueling or in the combat zone. But flying into the sun resulted in twenty hours of daylight, making a nap almost impossible. Sleep didn't matter, though, because they knew they were called on a mission bigger than themselves, and they pressed on with a warrior ethos.

As they approached the Pakistani coast from the south, the reality of the mission was setting in. Flexibility is the key to airpower, and Jethro needed it as 70 percent of the targets had changed according to updated intelligence on terrorist locations since they took off from Missouri. Airborne for thirty-five hours at this point, they had to program the JDAMs' coordinates into the B-2 via Combat Track II, which required thousands of keystrokes. With the help of some much-needed go-pills for focus, the pilots reprogrammed sixteen JDAMs in the two bomb bays. For two hours, they deployed on multiple ground targets, including aircraft, airfields, surface-to-air radars, and missile sites. These targets were critical to ensure air superiority and safe passage into Afghanistan for non-stealth USAF aircraft.

After the flawless destruction of thirteen targets, their monumental mission was still not over. They had egressed the combat zone low on gas and were headed for the last tanker when the Combined Air Operations Center informed them of a critical time-sensitive target (TST). Intelligence had ID'd additional high-value targets (HVTs) and these terrorists needed to be taken out. Following in-flight refueling, they headed back into the dark skies over enemy territory to attack four additional targets with the remaining JDAMs. At this point, they were all alone as the only aircraft left in country. They worked for one and a half hours and flawlessly destroyed the four targets. With the mission complete, they fenced out and air-refueled before finally landing in Diego Garcia after 44.3 hours in the air. Captain Neil and Major Deaile had just flown the longest combat sortie in history, but neither they nor anyone else would know that it would be just the beginning of the longest-running war in U.S. history.

As of February 2020, we have been fighting in Afghanistan for almost twenty years, with the high cost of 2,372 U.S. military deaths and over 20,000 wounded. Beyond the statistics, most will never see the aftereffects. The spouses and children left behind. The injuries sustained and those afflicted with PTSD. The emotional, mental, and physical turmoil.

One such example that is very personal to me is Major Larry Bauguess, whose legacy continues to inform my daily mission. On May 14, 2007, Major Bauguess was serving with the 82nd Airborne Division, deployed with his unit to Afghanistan in support of Operation Enduring Freedom. Bauguess and his commander crossed over the border into a tribal region of Pakistan with the goal of establishing a treaty along the unruly border. After a long and fruitful meeting, peace was negotiated and a treaty was reached. As the soldiers rallied to move back to the helicopter landing zone, instead of riding in the senior leader vehicles, Bauguess stayed behind with his men. As Major Bauguess climbed into the truck, a uniformed Pakistani Frontier Guardsman opened fire at close range. Bauguess shielded his men, taking the brunt of the assault. His selfless heroism would save the lives of his men but leave a wife and two young daughters without a husband and father to help raise them. Major Bauguess's wife, Wesley, is an Army veteran and understands the reality of war, but nothing can prepare you for that knock on the front door. *I just talked to him yesterday,* Wesley told herself as she worked up the will to open the door. *Yesterday was Mother's Day. This isn't happening.* But it did: The love of her life, Ryann and Ellie's hero, wasn't coming home.

Major Bauguess was buried with full military honors on May 20, 2007; a folded American flag was handed to Wesley and her girls. The official weight of the American burial flag is only 2.3 pounds, but it's a crushing symbolic weight to the families who must receive it. Folds of Honor is humbled to stand with Wesley, Ryann, and Ellie and help bear the weight of the flag by providing them an education in honor of their dad. It has been one of my greatest blessings to meet the heroic families we support and to bring them aboard as ambassadors of the greater Folds mission. Our effort is singular and unwavering: Honor the sacrifice and educate their legacy.

TOGETHER: 9/11

September 11, 2001, was a horrific day in American history. As humans, it's sometimes impossible to comprehend why terrible things happen, but God always finds ways to bring light to the darkest and most devastating of places. Though we didn't realize it at the time, a beautiful ray of light was placed upon us: We witnessed the best of the American spirit and were galvanized in ways we haven't been since World War II. Today, only nineteen years later, we seem so divided, separated by our politics, of which there are only two teams: the red team and the blue team. I pray that our nation can again find the spirit of red, white, and blue to come together and find a common ground.

In the same way that Jethro inspired us by flying the B-2 call sign "Spirit of America" on the longest combat mission in history, we, as Americans united by our differences, are bonded together by our struggles in search of happiness and fulfillment. This isn't always easy. I point again to the example of Wesley Bauguess. When Wesley was a second lieutenant serving in the 101st Airborne Division, her company commander, Captain Brian Gray, said, "Lieutenant Bauguess, in life you always have two choices. You can choose the easy wrong or the hard right." I pray that we may all choose the hard right on the path to CAVU.

I'VE GOT YOUR SIX: THE POWER OF HALLOWED WORDS

As fighter pilots, we use the clock position as a reference to point out other aircraft. Your "six" is the zone directly behind your jet, and the area most vulnerable to an undetected attack by an enemy aircraft. To protect against this we use a tactical formation called *line abreast,* in which two jets are separated by one and a half miles. This allows us the maximum flexibility to execute virtually any mission and affords each pilot with the best vantage point to clear the other pilot's six o'clock.

At Folds of Honor, we proudly tell our military families that we've "got your six." To date, there have been nearly two million dependents impacted by the death or permanent disability of a service member, and nine out of ten receive no federal education assistance. We will keep fighting to ensure we never leave a military family behind on the field of battle and in harm's way, always striving to have their six!

CALL TO DUTY

Fighter pilots receive a squadron coin after the successful completion of mission qualification training (MQT) at our first assigned squadron. MQT is the final evolution of our formal training that qualifies us as combat-ready wingmen. Getting the coin represents official entry into the fighter-pilot nation, a tradition whose origin dates back to the Great War. In 1917, American volunteers made up many of those in the squadrons that banded together in Europe before the United States officially entered World War I. These young warriors were a spirited fraternal group and made a special medallion that each pilot carried to identify themselves as a member of the squadron. The medallion proved invaluable for one young lieutenant during the war when he was shot down behind German lines and held as a POW in an outpost near the front lines. The American pilot eventually escaped and was recaptured by allied French soldiers, but at this point he had no uniform or identification to prove he was an American; the French sentenced him to death by firing squad. On his death march, he remembered the coin in his possession and promptly showed it to his captors, who stopped the execution order. Ever so apologetic, they gave him a bottle of Bordeaux instead.

Just like our brothers in arms from the Great War, we have stayed true to the tradition of the coin and "The Challenge." It works like this: Pilots can challenge each other by presenting their coin. If the other pilot presents their coin back, the challenger buys a drink; if they don't have their coin, they buy the drink. Yes, I have been caught without my coin a couple times in my career. An expensive lesson, but there's no one I would rather buy drinks for than my brothers in green flight suits.

JOIN THE MISSION OF FOLDS OF HONOR

In honor of our walk together, I would like to invite you to become a wingman for Folds of Honor. Please visit my website at Danrooney.com/coin and become a wingman at Folds of Honor. With a $13-per-month commitment to support military families, I will send you a personalized CAVU coin, thus making you an honorary wingman. To learn more about Folds of Honor and to join the mission, visit FoldsofHonor.org.

Danrooney.com and Folds of Honor are not affiliated with, endorsed or supported by HarperCollins.

Terms Only Fighter Pilots Understand

Angels: Altitude in thousands of feet. ("Angels 3" is 3,000 feet.)

Bandit: A known bad guy.

Bent: An inoperative piece of gear.

BFM: Basic fighter maneuvers. The 1v1 aircraft combat most commonly known as dogfighting. Gun kills are preferred.

Bingo: Low fuel status or a direction to head for the divert field. ("Lobo is bingo fuel," or "Ghostrider, your signal is bingo.")

Bitching Betty: The automated female voice that provides audible in-cockpit warnings in some fighter aircraft. She only has bad stuff to say.

Blind: Wingman not in sight.

Bogey: An unknown radar contact.

BOTOT: Bombs on time on target.

Bug out: To exit a dogfight rapidly. ("Gucci is on the bug.")

Buster: A direction to go as fast as possible.

BVR: Beyond visual range. The ability to engage an enemy aircraft prior to being able to see him.

CAS: Close air support. Supporting the troops on the ground by attacking ground targets.

CAVU: Ceiling and visibility unrestricted.

Cherubs: Altitude in hundreds of feet. ("Cherubs 3" is 300 feet.)

Chick: "Chicks in tow" describes fighters that are refueling in midair.

Code 3: An aircraft condition. If a jet is "Code 3," it requires maintenance action before it is safe for the next flight. A "Code 2" jet needs maintenance but is safe to fly. A "Code 1" jet is in perfect working order. These codes can describe other things like a pilot or your car. A pilot that is sick calls himself "Code 3."

Dead Bug: A fighter-pilot drinking game, usually in formal settings. Anytime the phrase "dead bug" is said, all pilots fall to the ground on their backs to resemble a dead bug.

Delta: To change to a later time, either minutes or hours depending on the context. ("Delta 10 on your recovery time" means the jet is now scheduled to land ten minutes later.)

DNIF: Duty Not Including/Involving Flying. The medical status of a pilot who is too sick to fly but can still perform other duties, as determined by the flight surgeon.

Dollar ride: The first flight of pilot training; you give your IP a decorated dollar bill as a thank-you. This is the only flight without the pressure of a grade sheet.

Doofer book: A storybook in which pilots recount mistakes in a humorous way. There are no rules about content or language. The only criterion is that the story must be at least 10 percent true.

FAIP: First Assignment Instructor Pilot. A pilot who graduates from pilot training whose first assignment is to return to pilot training as an instructor.

FEB: Flying Evaluation Board. Determines if you are safe to fly. An FEB can take away a pilot's wings.

Fence in/out: The procedure by which a fighter pilot sets his cockpit switches in order to prepare for combat. When he "crosses the fence," he "fences in" and sets his switches to the appropriate mode. He "fences out" when leaving.

Firewall: To push the throttles to their forward limit.

FNG: [Expletive] New Guy. The nickname given to

pilots who are new to a squadron and have not yet received a call sign.

Fox: A code word indicating the type of air-to-air missile that has been fired. "Fox 1" is semi-active radar missile (AIM-7 Sparrow); "Fox 2" is heat-seeking missile (AIM-9 Sidewinder); "Fox 3" is active radar missile (AIM-120 AMRAAM).

Fragged: An indication that the airplane is loaded weapons-wise according to the mission order. ("Devil 201 is on station as fragged.")

Frat: An abbreviation for fratricide—the killing of a friendly by a friendly (blue on blue), whether on the ground or in the air.

FUBAR: [Expletive] up beyond all recognition. My favorite bar at Eglin is actually called the FU BAR.

The Funky Chicken: What aviators call the involuntary movements that happen during G-LOC.

G: Gravity. Under one G, a pilot is in level flight and feels his normal weight. F-16s are capable of up to nine Gs. That feels like nine times your body weight.

G-LOC: G-induced loss of consciousness. A blackout caused by the loss of blood flow to the brain experienced by fighter pilots under high-G conditions.

Gouge: The "inside scoop." To have the answers or important information prior to an examination.

Grape: A pilot who's an easy kill in a dogfight.

Holding hands: Two fighters that are in a close formation.

Hook: To fail an upgrade flight. So called because of the hook-shaped U of "Unsatisfactory" that constitutes the grade of such a ride.

Jeremiah Weed: A terrible-tasting whiskey that is often the drink of choice for fighter pilots. It is kept in the freezer of a squadron bar or fighter pilot's home.

Naked: Radar warning gear lighting up without indication of a missile threat.

NASA: Call sign for a pilot having no (NA) situational awareness (SA).

Nose hot/cold: Usually used around the tanker pattern. An indication that the radar is or isn't transmitting.

Pickle: To expend ordnance. To "pickle" a bomb or "hit the pickle button" means to fire a weapon.

Pull chocks: To depart. The crew chief pulls the chocks, which are generally just wooden blocks painted yellow, out from the tires, allowing the aircraft to taxi. When a pilot is ready to depart (even if it's just to go home), he may say he's "pulling chocks."

Punch out: To eject from an airplane.

Queep: A term that is used to describe paperwork, reports, and other extraneous duties that keep a pilot out of the cockpit.

Redball: A request for maintenance response, generally when a pilot is starting up an aircraft to go on a mission. For instance, if a pilot has a radar problem, he will call, "Redball, radar," on the radio, which is a request for radar specialists.

Rolex: To change time over target.

RTB: Return to base. ("Big Eye, Eagle 301 is RTB.")

Sandbag: To "ride along" in the back seat of the two-seat version of a fighter, so called because single-seat fighter pilots generally don't like back-seaters and sometimes view them as nothing more than extra weight.

Shack: When a fighter pilot drops a bomb and makes a direct hit on a ground target.

Shelf check: Browsing at the local military exchange. So called particularly during deployments to austere locations, where people often go to the BX/PX to see what's for sale not because they need something, but because it's "something to do."

Sierra Hotel: Phonetic pronunciation of "S.H.," which stands for "shit hot." This is the highest compliment you can receive as a fighter pilot.

Situational awareness: SA. The ability to know and understand what has happened, what is happening, and what will happen, as well as where you are in time and space. By the time loss of SA is recognized, it has been gone for some time.

So to speak: STS. A fighter-pilot expression that follows any phrase that may in some way be construed as having a sexual connotation.

Spiked: Um, not that "spiked." The real "spiked" is an indication of a missile threat on the radar warning receiver. ("Rooster has an SA-6 spike at three o'clock.")

Tally: Enemy in sight (as opposed to "visual," which means friendly in sight). ("Nuke is tally two bandits, four o'clock low.")

Tango Uniform: Phonetic pronunciation of "T.U.," literally, "tits up." Something that is Tango Uniform is dead, inoperative, broken, or otherwise malfunctioning.

Texaco: Either a label for the tanker or direction to go to the tanker.

Tumbleweed: When a pilot has a complete loss of situational awareness. Often occurs when a wingman is so confused that all he can do is stay visual with his flight lead and hope he'll eventually figure out what's going on.

Vapes: The condensation cloud created when an airplane pulls a lot of Gs.

Visual: Wingman (or other friendly) in sight (as opposed to "tally," which means enemy in sight). ("Weezer, you got me?" "Roger, Weezer is visual.")

Winchester: Out of weapons.

WOM: Word of mouth. A WOM is generally an action or "rule" that is consistently quoted but no one can find any regulation to support it.

Acknowledgments

I hope that while reading *Fly Into the Wind* you heard one message loud and clear: I didn't achieve CAVU without the incredible wingmen in my life. I can't include everyone in the book but wanted to ensure I recognized the heroes of faith in my life. My family is first on the list. Jacqy and my girls, Victoria, Tatum, Mia, Reese, and Devyn, sacrifice so much time with Dad so we can support other military families. I love you. Mom and Dad, who are always there to talk and have never stopped sharing life advice and unwavering support. My sisters, Beth and Kate, are awesome siblings.

Thank you to the amazing team at Folds of Honor for the heroic work that you do. A special salute to Ben Leslie and Col Nick Nichols. Our board members for their tireless advocacy, Mike "Silk" Arbour, Chris

Williams, Brian Whitcomb, Ryan Lewellyn, Larry Pfeiffer, Jeff Babineau, Chuck Odell, and Johnny Powers. To all the early believers in Folds of Honor whose support pushed me to keep going, Presidents Bush 41 and 43, Rickie Fowler, Jim Nance, Gary Woodland, David Feherty, Roger Schiffman, Dave Novak, Vince Gill, Brian O'Connell, Dierks Bentley, and Joe Steranka.

To the PGA of America and all my fellow professionals who made Patriot Golf Day possible. Thank you, Seth Waugh, for ensuring that Folds and the PGA stay together for the long haul. Thank you to team America at The Patriot, who saved me from bankruptcy, and the coalition that came together at American Dunes: Jack Nicklaus, Scott Tolley, Chris Cochran, Ryan Lewellyn, George Rusu, Nick Hentges, Mike and Dina Dargis, Doug Bell, Dave North, Bill Duval, Perry Schmidt, and all my hole sponsors for being driving forces at American Dunes.

Johnny Sap, Augie, Bob Philion, and Dan Ladd for making Volition America a reality and staying the course. Harry Rhodes and Christine Farrell at Washington Speakers Bureau for providing me with a platform to share the Folds of Honor story. Paul Brothers, for all the amazing brand work you have done for me and Folds. To all our supporters and true friends at Fox News, Brian

Kilmeade, Ainsley Earheart, Pete and Jen Hegseth, Lauren Petterson, Sean Hannity, Tucker Carlson, Ed Henry, Dan Bongino, Anna Kooiman, Lynda McLaughlin, and my brother in Christ Gavin Hadden for connecting all the relationships.

To all the fighter pilots in the 138th: a special thank-you for your mentorship to Col Rookie Rooks, Col Otter Stratton, Gen Bud Wyatt, Gen Mark Welsh, Col Mike Loforti, and Gen Steve Cortright. To my current squadron bros in the 301st: your support and fellowship are one of the greatest blessings in my life. Thank you, Major Rob "Shotz" Burgon, for your research on this book.

Thank you to all those who helped me put my soul on paper. My editor, Matthew Daddona, for always pushing for more, and Paula Balzer, for helping me find the right words. Jacqy, for always making sure my voice was genuine. Thank you, Steve Doocy—who would have guessed that my mom's chicken noodle recipe in your cookbook would lead to an introduction to HarperCollins? Thank you to Dr. Dave Cook for introducing me to the power of volition. Finally, thank you to Danica Patrick, Sean Hannity, Jack Nicklaus, and Gary Woodland for providing quotes for the book.

Bibliography

Achenbach, Joel. "Apollo 8: NASA's First Moonshot Was a Bold and Terrifying Improvisation." *Washington Post,* June 18, 2019, www.washingtonpost.com /history/2018/12/20/apollo-nasas-first-moonshot-was -bold-terrifying-improvisation.

Cassidy, Jessica. "Why One Act of Kindness Is Usually Followed by Another." *Goodnet,* November 23, 2015, www.goodnet.org/articles/one-act-kindness-usually -followed-by-another.

Derbyshire, Emma J. "Flexitarian Diets and Health: A Review of the Evidence-Based Literature." *Frontiers in Nutrition* 3, no. 55 (2016), www.ncbi.nlm.nih.gov /pmc/articles/PMC5216044/.

Freston, Kathy. "A Vegan Diet (Hugely) Helpful Against

Cancer." Huffpost, December 9, 2012, www.huffpost
.com/entry/vegan-diet-cancer_b_2250052.

"General Orders, 3 August 1776." *Founders Online*,
National Archives, accessed March 18, 2020, https://
founders.archives.gov/documents/Washington/03
-05-02-0415. [Original source: *The Papers of George
Washington*. Revolutionary War Series, vol. 5, 16
June 1776–12 August 1776, ed. Philander D. Chase.
Charlottesville: University Press of Virginia, 1993,
pp. 551–552.]

Landis, K. R., J. S. House, and D. Umberson. "Social
Relationships and Health." *Science* 241, no. 4685
(July 29, 1988), science.sciencemag.org/content/241
/4865/540.

Lerner, Preston. "Bob Pardo Once Pushed a Crippled
F-4 Home with His F-4. In Flight." *Air & Space*,
March 21, 2017, www.airspacemag.com/military
-aviation/pardos-push-180962402.

Mineo, Liz. "Over Nearly 80 Years, Harvard Study Has
Been Showing How to Live a Healthy and Happy
Life." *Harvard Gazette*, November 26 2018, news
.harvard.edu/gazette/story/2017/04/over-nearly-80
-years-harvard-study-has-been-showing-how-to-live
-a-healthy-and-happy-life.

Poulin, Michael J., et al. "Giving to Others and the Association Between Stress and Mortality." *American*

Journal of Public Health 103, no. 9 (September 2013), ajph.aphapublications.org/doi/full/10.2105/AJPH .2012.300876.

Shane, Leo. "New Veteran Suicide Numbers Raise Concerns Among Experts Hoping for Positive News." *Military Times,* October 9, 2019, www.militarytimes.com /news/pentagon-congress/2019/10/09/new-veteran -suicide-numbers-raise-concerns-among-experts -hoping-for-positive-news.

Watson, Stephanie. "Volunteering May Be Good for Body and Mind." *Harvard Health Blog,* October 30, 2015, www.health.harvard.edu/blog/volunteering-may-be -good-for-body-and-mind-201306266428.

Weinfuss, Josh. "Amazing Amy: Meet Gary Woodland's U.S. Open Inspiration." ESPN, June 19, 2019, www.espn.com/golf/story/_/id/27003863/meet -amazing-amy-bockerstette-gary-woodland-us-open -inspiration.

Wentling, Nikki. "VA Says Veteran Suicide Rate Is 17 Per Day After Change in Calculation." *Stars and Stripes,* September 20, 2019, www.stripes.com/news/us/va -says-veteran-suicide-rate-is-17-per-day-after-change -in-calculation-1.599857.

Wiest, Brianna. "12 Daily Routines of Famous People in History—And What You Should Take from Each." *Thought Catalog,* February 22, 2019, thoughtcatalog

.com/brianna-wiest/2015/11/12-daily-routines-of
-famous-people-in-history-and-what-you-should-take
-from-each.

Wormley, Rob. "The Schedules of 20 Famous People,
Past & Present [Infographic]." *When I Work,* October 24, 2017, wheniwork.com/blog/famous-people
-schedules-infographic.

About the Author

Lieutenant Colonel Dan Rooney is the founder of the Folds of Honor Foundation; an F-16 fighter pilot with nearly 2,000 hours of flight time and three combat tours in Iraq; and a PGA Professional. He founded The Patriot Golf Club and the American Dunes Golf Club and is the author of *A Patriot's Calling: My Life as an F-16 Fighter Pilot.*

Rooney is a professional speaker represented exclusively by Washington Speakers Bureau. He was the motivational team speaker for two U.S. Ryder Cup teams. From humble beginnings above his garage, Lt Colonel Rooney started the nonprofit Folds of Honor. Its singular mission is to provide educational scholarships to the spouses and children of wounded or killed-in-action military service members. In twelve years, Folds of Honor has provided twenty-five thousand life-changing scholarships totaling more than $125 million.

Lt Colonel Rooney is also a decorated military aviator: He is a two-time recipient of the Top Gun award and was honored with the Spirit of Attack award as a top graduate of F-16 training. He has received many decorations, including the Air Force Commendation Medal, Air Medal, Global War on Terrorism Service Medal, Combat Readiness Medal, and Air Expeditionary Medal. Lt Colonel Rooney continues to fly fighters as an aggressor pilot in the 301st Fighter Squadron at Eglin Air Force Base in Destin, Florida. For his service and patriotism, he was presented the White House's Volunteer Service Award by President George W. Bush, the Air National Guard's Distinguished Service Medal and Directors Service Award, and the Ellis Island Medal of Honor.

Rooney is a Kansas University Distinguished Alumni, Significant Sigma Chi, and recipient of the Oklahoma Medal of Freedom. He was honored at the Masters invitational with the William D. Richardson Award for his outstanding contributions to golf, and he received the PGA of America's first-ever Patriot Award. He has been recognized as one of *People* magazine's Heroes of the Year, *Money* magazine's Hero of the Year, and ABC *World News Tonight*'s Person of the Year. He was a CNN Hero and was awarded the Fox Nation Ultimate Patriot Award.

He lives in Owasso, Oklahoma, with his wife, five daughters, and three dogs.

HARPER
LARGE PRINT

We hope you enjoyed reading
our new, comfortable print size and found it
an experience you would like to repeat.

Well – you're in luck!

Harper Large Print offers the finest in
fiction and nonfiction books in this same larger
print size and paperback format. Light and easy to read,
Harper Large Print paperbacks are for the book lovers
who want to see what they are reading without strain.

For a full listing of titles and
new releases to come, please visit our website:
www.hc.com

HARPER LARGE PRINT